Religion-less Christianity and Renewing the Church

On Being a Follower of Jesus… in God, for God, without God

Johan Bergh

Copyright © 2018 Johan Bergh
All rights reserved.
ISBN:9781720014010

DEDICATION

I dedicate this work to all those whose world-view embraces 21st century science and culture and whose faith-view embraces Jesus of the 1st century as real and life-changing for how we can live and thrive in these days, and to all who work toward the church of Jesus being and doing the way of Jesus for the world: peace by distributive justice through non-violence.

CONTENTS

1 **Introduction**

2 **Religion-less Christianity = trust and self-giving (faith and love) within a "World-Come-Of-Age Consciousness" rather than a "Religious Consciousness"** — Pg 6

3 **A Look at Christianity That Lives Within a Religious Consciousness** — Pg 18

4 **What Church Renewal Looks Like Today Within the Religious Consciousness** — Pg 29

5 **What Church Renewal Looks Like Today In A Religion-less Christianity** — Pg 36

6 **Conclusion** — Pg 49

7 **Appendix Part One**
Journal Jottings on Religion-less Christianity December 2017 – July 2018 — Pg 52

8 **Appendix Part Two**
Life Together E-Letter Postings January – May 2018 — Pg 70

1

Introduction

The challenge to be addressed: the gospel of Jesus Christ has been domesticated to being a balm for our pathologies and corrupted to being a support for our personal and corporate projects. The church of Jesus Christ is declining in numbers and relevance.

The focus of this work: it may be possible for us to see and use Dietrich Bonhoeffer's work on "religion-less Christianity" to build not only a theology to bring the gospel to being the good news of Jesus the Nazarene but also an ecclesiology to give the church a way of being a missional community in this new day.

Some background: I embarked on a Sabbatical in 2018 and a significant portion of the plan for the sabbatical was to reflect on Dietrich Bonhoeffer's writing on "religion-less Christianity."

At the beginning of the year I took the opportunity of using my weekly e-letter to my congregation (St. Philip Lutheran Church, Mt. Dora, Florida), entitled "Life Together," to write reflections specifically on the topic (religion-less Christianity). In my daily journaling I found myself writing any number of pieces on the topic as well.

All of these reflections, "Life Together" postings and daily journal entries, have been compiled as "grist for the mill" and "conversation starters" on the topic and are available here as appendixes.

I came to realize that I wanted to explore how specifically how a religion-less Christianity could address the need we have today for a renewed church.

What we have here is certainly not exhaustive and is not intended to be comprehensive. In fact, it beckons further development and I welcome feedback and input.

And one more thing: it likely does exactly what Ernst Feil in his key book on Bonhoeffer's theology warned us about: I am likely "over-interpreting" Bonhoeffer by building too much of an understanding of church life and practice (ecclesiology) if not also Jesus Christ (Christology) from a development of thought (religion-less Christianity) that was left undeveloped by Bonhoeffer's death.1 But, over-interpret I will, because the church today needs a way forward in renewal that is full of reality, full of world, full of Jesus and full of faith.

So, on to the topic at hand:

First, how "religion-less Christianity" can be defined by contrasting "world come of age consciousness" to "religious consciousness."

Secondly, a look at Christianity that lives within a religious consciousness.

---

1 Feil, Ernst, *The Theology of Dietrich Bonhoeffer* (Minneapolis, MN: Fortress Press, 1985), 3. Feil: "If one builds an argument on the basis of those letters (sic: *Letters and Papers from Prison*), one becomes open to the charge of over-interpreting Bonhoeffer.
If on the other hand the central assertions of *Letters and Papers from Prison* are regarded as theologically very relevant despite the fact that they have not been developed in detail, then one fashions the key to interpretation from Bonhoeffer's biography and supports this procedure with the claim that a consideration of both his life and work together is requisite to an understanding of him."

Thirdly, a look at what church renewal looks like and seeks to achieve and does so within a religious consciousness.

Lastly, what church renewal looks like in a religion-less Christianity and a world-come-of-age consciousness.

2

Religion-less Christianity = trust and self-giving (faith and love) within a "World-Come-Of-Age Consciousness" rather than a "Religious Consciousness"

To begin: coming to understand religion-less Christianity by contrasting a world-come-of-age consciousness with a religious consciousness.

Larry Rasmussen in *Dietrich Bonhoeffer: His Significance for North Americans*, gives a helpful overview of the relationship of a "religious" vs. a "world-come-of-age" consciousness2.

The characteristics we can give religious consciousness are as follows: 1) God is a supernatural being if not simply a theological

---

2 Rasmussen, Larry and Bethge, Renate, *Dietrich Bonhoeffer: His Significance for North Americans* (Eugene, Oregon: Wipf and Stock Publishers, 2016), 62.

hypothesis to explain all the unexplainable things in life 2) God is a "deus ex machina," a supernatural being who is called upon to be involved and intervene in human affairs to correct or make right what has gone wrong.

In relation to #1 above, God as supernatural being and/or theological hypotheses to explain the unexplainable, we contrast a world-come-of-age consciousness which knows nothing of a supernatural being that exists or is needed to answer or solve life's questions or challenges. In a world come of age the key characteristic is "the growth of human autonomy through the increase of human knowledge and powers. Humankind in a world come of age, using its autonomous reason, can and does interpret natural and social processes and can and does face and answer life's questions without the tutelage of a divinity, that is, from premises that need not and do not posit God.3

---

3 IBID, 63.

Religion in a religious consciousness becomes marginalized, ironically enough, because God is only necessary for those areas of life that are problematic.

In the development of what is known as "The Wholeness Wheel"[4] we see a helpful illustration of a religious consciousness transforming to a world-come-of-age consciousness where religion moves from being a portion of life, and perhaps there an ever increasingly smaller portion of life, to the very definition of every dimension of life.

Some years back, in its early iteration, The Wholeness Wheel had the following sections in the "pie" or "wheel" diagram, as best as I can remember, that labeled dimension of life: intellectual, emotional, relational, physical, spiritual. Evidently for those working with this illustration, something seemed lacking or skewed.

---

[4] www.porticobenefits.org, Portico Benefits Services, A Ministry of the Evangelical Lutheran Church in America. See "Called to Live Well" and "Wellness Resources" for The Wholeness Wheel.

The "wheel" was updated, and happily so, because not only was something key to so much of life added as a section of the wheel, a piece of the pie, but most interestingly and germane for our discussion here, something was taken out as a section, a piece, and placed in the illustration in a way that demonstrates its full and actual place. What was added was "financial," and what was taken out as a "section" or "piece of the pie" was "spiritual." It's this latter move that interests us here. Where was the "spiritual" dimension of life placed now in this illustration? It was taken out as a section or piece and placed as the actual circle on the wheel, crust-rim of the pie. "Spiritual" went from being a part of life that gets addressed on occasion to being the very whole of life that is expressed in every dimension, section, piece of the pie, of life. The wellness sections of the Wholeness Wheel today are: emotional, physical, intellectual, financial, inter-personal/social. And now the "spiritual well-being" wraps itself around all of these dimensions of life and impacts every dimension.

And, perhaps, more profoundly and more challenging for our religious consciousness, in a world-come-of-age consciousness it is not a separate dimension around the wheel that touches and influences all sections within the wheel but rather a way of describing the truest expression of each of the parts of life. The Financial is not impacted by The Spiritual. Financial *is* Spiritual. Emotional is not impacted by Spiritual. Emotional *is* Spiritual. And so on.

So, in the current format, the Wholeness Wheel can be a helpful picture for how the world-come-of-age consciousness actually functions: The divine, be it God or however the supernatural is identified, is not called upon to intersect with the human when the human dimensions of life are troubled or in need of help. The divine is already there and fully functioning within the very human and earthly enterprises that are our life. The divine is not a portion, it is the whole. The divine does not diminish human autonomy or call it into question. It does not sit on the sidelines waiting for weakness to show up so it can act. Rather, it is the center of all activity, and is as much a part of human and earthly strength as it is the weakness.

Let's move on to the second characteristic we have identified for religious consciousness: the "deus ex machina." Rasmussen writes,

"In plays of antiquity, whenever the normal course of human events simply could not muster some action essential to the plot, a god or goddess intervened and did his or her job. The business of life and the plot could then move on to the next dramatic episode.

*Bonhoeffer contends that people of religious consciousness turn to God and religion only (but always) when their human resources fail to secure 'solutions' to problems that exhaust them or that they regard (or choose to regard) as insoluble or interminable. God and religion 'rescue' us from dangers we encounter but cannot face or control."*5

In contrast, in a world-come-of-age consciousness, God is not an option. Human autonomy and human intelligence and experience are not only significant, they are the singular way in which human events are engaged. There may and will be failures and/or struggles to find a way forward in the human project, but there is no reverting to a problem-solver out of the temporal domain.

---

5 Rasmussen, Larry and Bethge, Renate, *Dietrich Bonhoeffer: His Significance for North Americans* (Eugene, Oregon: Wipf and Stock Publishers, 2016), 63-64.

Bonhoeffer sought to engage a life of faith with a world-come-of-age consciousness.

He rejected a religion that saw persons as the center and God on the periphery where God was called upon to assist the human endeavors, however laudable, or where God was called upon to redeem human failures, however actual. "He laments such religion and he applauds the world's coming of age."6 Instead, he saw faith as the experience where God is at the center of all things, good and bad and indifferent, and God is trusted (faith) and followed (love).

It might be a good idea to comment here about this world-come-of-age consciousness and its experience of faith in God and how this relates to the very common conversations these days about so many people walking away from "religion" but who like to engage many ideas and practices they deem "spiritual." Unfortunately, what happens more than not is that folks who believe they are now engaging "spirituality" instead of "religion" have more or less simply acquired another form of religion as we have defined it here.

---

6 IBID, 65

When people state they are tired of "religion" but they still believe in God and are thus "spiritual," what they normally mean is not that they are tired of religion (God is the supernatural that explains the unexplainable and God is the "deus ex machina") but rather that they are tired of religious practices (e.g. worship services, prayers, church membership and its requirements) and want to find or experience the God of religion (again, supernatural rescuer) in some more palatable if not enjoyable format. Most folks today are tired of the way of being religious but they are not tired of religion. What Bonhoeffer was getting at with a "religion-less Christianity" was dropping any psychological, moral or theological pretense of being able as humanity to approach or make our way to God or anything we might want from God. Bonhoeffer was tired of religion, not religious practices. Being "religion-less" is not about not doing traditional "church," or even, for that matter, not agreeing with the social justice positions of much of today's church (e.g. gay marriage, death penalty, abortion, environmental concerns).

Ernst Feil states, "What is quite clear already is that a religion-less Christianity is not simply one which no longer exercises what are traditionally known as religious practices, such as prayer, Bible study, sermon, communion, common life, and not least, confession."[7]

It's clear to me, however, and I will try to address this in the last chapter, that while we don't want to confuse religion with religious practices, we clearly also need to reform or renew our religious practices (and keep working on social justice) to engage folks today who simply don't connect anymore to the traditional practices and don't connect anymore to a church who turns its back on racial, economic, gender and environmental injustice. And then, to make a finer point on the why of all of this "engaging folks today": we don't do this because they need God for a better life. We do this because God needs them for a better world.

---

[7] Feil, Ernst, *The Theology of Dietrich Bonhoeffer* (Minneapolis, MN: Fortress Press, 1985), 161.

Turning from a religious consciousness to a world-come-of-age consciousness, then, is not a matter of changing spiritual practices within the same religion. A little more here on that. In an August 5, 2018 *New York Times Sunday Review* column, writer Molly Worthen describes how there is a growing phenomenon she calls the "Podcast Bros" where any number of podcasters are espousing techniques for daily living so that listeners can change their lives and fulfill their human potential for happiness and well-being. Worthen notes what many have chronicled: many folks are disillusioned with church and traditional religious life and like engaging their life's possibilities unfettered from the restrictions of traditional church: "…over the past few years the podcasters have become a significant cultural phenomenon, spiritual entrepreneurs who are filling the gap left as traditional religious organizations erode and modernity frays our face-to-face connections with communities and institutions."

Finding identity, belonging, and meaning outside of church life, even for those who grew up in church life, is more and more the case and the podcast communities certainly don't have a corner on church alternatives, but I cite this podcasting community as an illustration of a religious consciousness that is the same as the traditional church: the focus is on the person as Subject who then does the reaching out and engaging of whatever Help is available, be that "self-help" or "divine help," in order to achieve said person's goals and aspirations. Worthen again: "Don't dismiss the podcast bros merely as hucksters promoting self-help books and dubious mushroom coffee. In this secularized age of lonely seekers scrolling social media feeds, they have cultivated a spiritual community. They offer theologies and daily rituals of self-actualization, an appealing alternative to the rhetoric of victimhood and resentment that permeates both the right and the left." I don't dismiss the "bros" or any other alternatives to traditional church. They in fact may be more authentically community than many a church community. But that is not my concern here.

It is this: their efforts at identity and meaning and self-actualization if not also community well-being are as religious as traditional church: help is needed and help is accessible and help can be applied when all other methods and life circumstances fail.

To conclude, then, our definition of religion-less Christianity by contrasting religious consciousness with world-come-of-age consciousness, we might define a religion-less Christianity as faith centered in Christ in a life totally immersed and involved in creation (the day to day of work, play, relationships). Religion-less Christianity is a faith that does not see Christ as the answer to our questions of identity, community, meaning and destiny but rather sees Christ as the question to our answers of identity, community, meaning and destiny.

A religion-less Christianity trusts Christ to listen, guide, direct, forgive, renew but does not rely on Christ to fill in our gaps of knowledge or solutions.

3

A Look at Christianity That Lives Within a Religious Consciousness

John Dominic Crossan, in *The Greatest Prayer*, helpfully identifies the types of prayers we find when we engage the book of Psalms in the Bible. He finds two major groupings within the 150 Psalms: 1) Request: request and petition 2) Gratitude: thanksgiving and praise.

When you read through the Psalms you can see these readily enough. But Crossan goes on to suggest that the prayers of the Psalms are not the only types we find the Bible and in fact are not the most developed or mature. There is a third: Empowerment, participation and collaboration.[8] He suggests there is a movement from Request to Gratitude to Empowerment and that these 3 categories are not arbitrarily numbered. They are sequential in how

---

8 Crossan, John Dominic, *The Greatest Prayer: Rediscovering the Revolutionary Message of The Lord's Prayer* (New York, NY: Harper Collins, 2010), 27

a person normally grows and develops in engaging the Divine in conversation.

The most fundamental communication: we call on the Supernatural, however we define it, to intervene and aid the natural. We ask for help for ourselves and others. Secondly, we not only say "please" but also "thank you." In our gratitude for assistance, on whatever level, we give thanks and praise to the one who helps. There is reason to appreciate these first two levels, if you will, of prayer, not only as the beginnings of a relationship with the divine but as levels that we never outgrow nor should be necessarily try to outgrow. No matter how mature, in fact it can be argued, only the mature, recognize the need for help and the gift of appreciation. That being said, there is more to prayer than Request and Gratitude. There is Empowerment. In fact, one could argue, and Crossan does, that without the prayer of Empowerment there is really no conversation, no relationship, with God at all.

Crossan turns to the prophets to tell how we are brought here.9 Amos, Hosea, Micah and First Isaiah of the 8th Century B.C.E., Jeremiah of the 7th century B.C.E., and Third Isaiah of the 6th century B.C.E. all rip into the people of Israel and Judah for paying attention to worship and rituals of piety while neglecting the care and well-being of the poor and marginalized. Amos 5:21-24 is representative. God is speaking: *"I hate, I despise your festivals, and I take no delight in your solemn assemblies. Even though you offer me your burnt offerings and grain offerings, I will not accept them; and the offerings of well-being of your fatted animals I will not look upon. Take away from me the noise of your songs; I will not listen to the melody of your harps. But let justice roll down like waters, and righteousness like and ever-flowing stream."*

There is a "both-and" dynamic that exists between the Psalms and the Prophets, between prayer and action.

The criticism of prayer that is empty of action is not to diminish the importance of prayer, it is to lift up the nature of prayer as

---
9 IBID, 13 ff.

complete only when the neighbor and creation are being served. Psalms and Prophets, Prayer and Action, are not two separate movements that must find each other, they are rather two sides to the one coin that is life in and through God.

Again, Crossan:

"But my proposal is that, although those two aspects of biblical religion can be distinguished, they cannot be separated. The twin sides of a coin, I repeat, cannot be separated without both sides being destroyed.
You may prefer heads to tails or tails to heads, but if you attempt to have only one of them, you will end up with neither. On the one hand, since God is a God of justice, you cannot pray to such a God in a state of injustice – not, at least without insincerity or even hypocrisy. On the other, to pray sincerely and with integrity to such a God risks empowerment by that God for that same justice."[10]

Seeing this kind of relationship, this ebb and flow, between prayer and action, reflected in the biblical materials can help us see that a religious consciousness that turns to God for intervention has been around a long time. Perhaps always.

Today's church has built its religious consciousness from portions of the biblical testimony and has not been able to engage well the two sides of the coin nor adapt and engage a world-come-of-age

---

[10] Crossan, John Dominic, *The Greatest Prayer: Rediscovering the Revolutionary Message of The Lord's Prayer* (New York, NY: Harper Collins, 2010), 20

where human autonomy and knowledge have relegated the supernatural to the superstitious.

Without much difficulty we can see how Request and Gratitude match up well with a Religious Consciousness: the divine exists to help when all else fails (even if we believe all attempts at success, temporally or heavenly, are sinfully so). I'd like to suggest that the third grouping, Empowerment, fits well with a world-come-of-age consciousness. Remember that the world-come-of-age consciousness sees no particular place nor necessity for any assistance from a supernatural source. While the Psalms of course do in fact engage the divine, the Prophets do so with a particular expectation that human responsibility and accountability are the key to the efficacy of the prayer.

Much of contemporary church lives out of a religious consciousness: we turn to God for answers and solutions to our problems and challenges and the reason for church, being involved in church, is to invoke God as the saving help to the dilemmas as we define them. While there is reason for prayer that is filled with Request and Gratitude, without the dimension of Empowerment there is not only a stunted biblical theology but there is little opportunity to allow God to speak at all to the many who in a world-come-of-age consciousness dismiss the divine as superfluous.

There is a maturity in the relationship with God that is one of empowerment, that lives a faith with a world-come-of-age consciousness. I'm reminded of the research that Willowcreek Church (Chicago area, non-denominational) did a number of years ago as they analyzed why in their 'mega-church' so many people were coming and then leaving over the years. What they saw is that in the development of an individual Christian, there are at least three major phases of growth. They found that the first two were widely experienced and recognizable in their congregation 1) coming to know Christ 2) relying on Christ for help for yourself and others.

It was the third phase, the most mature if you will, that they found lacking in significant ways in their congregation: seeing your life of faith as you helping Christ help others. The maturation comes in coming to a point in your faith where God is not here for you, rather, you are here for God. What Willowcreek decided is that they needed to help people get to the 3rd phase, the most mature phase, of a relationship with God in order to have people come to be a part of the church and not walk away when the going got rough, when things didn't happen in their life the way they wanted them to happen. What I see in this Willowcreek analysis of their own church life is a sober and honest appraisal of how we in the church live out of a religious consciousness for most of what we do: we appreciate seeing the value of God for us and in fact, most religious leaders as they say they are preaching and teaching the Gospel sound like they are the business of selling the value of God to customers so that people will sign up and join their church business.

There is another significant influence on directing us to a religious consciousness that too, like the recognition and use of "Request" and "Gratitude" in biblical testimony without an equally strong life of "Empowerment," comes from an incomplete if not stunted biblical theology. It is our atonement theologies, our understanding of just why and how Jesus does his saving work. Recognizing the at least three major working atonement theologies and how they each represent Christ as savior is work done by others and cannot be detailed here.[11] That being said, it is the so-called "Sacrificial Atonement" or "Substitution Atonement" theology that has been the most influential and practiced theology in the Western Church over the last 200 years and that, I believe, is a key source in directing us and keeping us in a religious consciousness. Briefly, the Substitution/Sacrifice atonement teaching sees Christ as helping us out of the problem of being an affront to God for our disobedience and distrust. We have a problem: sin. God has a solution: Jesus.

---

[11] One of the best recent works that I have found is *Making Sense of the Cross* by David Lose. I commend it to you and urge you to be familiar with all 3 major theologies we have employed throughout the 2000 years of Christianity. Then, too, most importantly, Lose lays out the groundwork for what is now in these days a fourth, and in my view, most biblical theology that can and does honestly engage Christ with a world-come-of-age consciousness.

It doesn't take long to see how Jesus, in this theology, is an answer to a problem that to many does not exist. In a world-come-of-age consciousness the ramifications and impacts of human failings call out for a human accountability and responsibility, not for a divine intervention. Instead of the church today working hard to engage honestly this world-come-of-age consciousness, it has spent most of its time trying to convince those with a world-come-of-age consciousness that they simply are myopic and need to come to their senses (!) and see who they really are: people who need God. Instead of engaging the life, death and resurrection of Jesus testimony from a world-come-of-age consciousness, the church holds on to a religious consciousness that simply doesn't compute for most people today.

There are signs of hope, significantly so: a "Fourth" atonement theology is emerging: one one could be called "event and experience," one that attempts to look at what actually happened to and with Jesus and come to conclusions for us as we live in a world no longer calling for supernatural intervention.12

---

12 Again, I direct you to *Making Sense of the Cross*, David Lose well as, for that matter, the entire

To state the case on how we in the church today not only passively resist engaging a world-come-of-age consciousness but actively so, I turn to helpful words from Rasmussen on Bonhoeffer (which includes a quote from Bonhoeffer):

"[Bonhoeffer] laments such religion and applauds the world's coming of age. Thus he laments religious Christianity and religious worship, and calls for religion-less Christianity and the 'non-religious interpretation of biblical concepts.'
Bonhoeffer is aware that a certain irony and tragedy wait on the wings. The church will fight the world's coming of age and do all in its power to save a place for God and religion. The clergy will, in Bonhoeffer's language, use all their 'clerical tricks' to retain religion as a sector of life. They will do this by marketing certain questions and problems – death and guilt, for example – 'to which [supposedly] only God can give an answer.' The irony is that world-come-of-age people are, in their godlessness, actually closer to confronting the God of the Bible who calls people to become fully responsible for their world, than are religious Christians and the church in their alliance with the 'God' of religion. The tragedy is that the church will be the strongest opponent of the rediscovery of Christianity in its nonreligious biblical roots and will be the able opponent of its own conversion (conversion here means a deeply altered consciousness). Bonhoeffer's language is anything but timid.
'The attack by Christian apologetics on the adulthood of the world I consider to be in the first place pointless, in the second place ignoble, and in the third place unchristian. Pointless, because it seems to me like an attempt to put a grown-up back into adolescence, i.e. to make him dependent, and thrusting him into problems that are, in fact, no longer problems to him. Ignoble, because it amounts to an attempt to exploit man's weakness for purposes that are alien to him and to which he has not freely assented.

---

works of Marcus Borg and John Dominic Crossan.

Unchristian, because it confuses Christ with one particular stage in man's religiousness, i.e. with human law.'"[13]

What I have attempted to do here is simply describe at least two of the significant influences on church today that work to keep us in a religious consciousness and a religious Christianity: one, the biblical theology of prayer that lacks the prophetic, and two, the systematic theology of atonement that lacks the actual event and experience of the first century Jesus and his followers.

---

[13] Rasmussen, Larry and Bethge, Renate, *Dietrich Bonhoeffer: His Significance for North Americans* (Eugene, Oregon: Wipf and Stock Publishers, 2016), 65-66.

4

What Church Renewal Looks Like Today Within
the Religious Consciousness

The key point I want to relate here is that all the church renewal work that I have seen over the past 40 years has been an attempt to make a church with a Religious Consciousness more acceptable and meaningful and engaging and that, not only is this less and less interesting to the de-churched folks over these years but it is also a lost cause and a misdirected use, if not abuse, of the Gospel with unchurched folk who live in a world-come-of-age consciousness. Lost cause, because like Bonhoeffer noted in what I shared above, one cannot put reason and the scientific method "back in the bottle" from whence it has come (as much as the church has tried to do so).

And misdirected or abuse of Gospel because the good news is that grace reigns in and through Christ Jesus and peace is to be experienced by distributive justice through non-violence and not that judgment reigns in and through our beliefs and behaviors and peace is to be experienced by victory through violence.

What we need is church renewal with and through a World-Come-of Age Consciousness and a Religion-less Christianity. We'll take a look at just what that might look like in our last chapter, but first we take a few minutes to unpack just what church renewal has looked like with and through a Religious Consciousness and a Religion Christianity.

It has been widely chronicled elsewhere how steep the decline in church worship attendance, overall church involvement and membership in these days. 14

14https://www.google.com/search?q=church+attendance+statistics+last+100+years&tbm=isch&source=iu&ictx=1&fir=K8tlKR-pHU9NBM%253A%252CfnrIU8WeY5kRLM%252C_&usg=AFrqEzdw7_a7DyG8jCfPklMNWDXR5P6q2g&sa=X&ved=2ahUKEwiy7LbB6eXcAhXKMd8KHUEOBUIQ9QEwAnoECAIQCA#imgrc=K8tlKR-pHU9NBM:

I have been in mission development, working to grow the mission of God, for 37 years, as a congregational Pastor. When I first started out the church at large was just beginning to feel the decline after the hay days of the mid-20th century. The church growth movement was kicking in and the "missio dei" understanding of mission being not to grow the church but rather for the church to grow the mission of God, was in its infancy. There were years of the artificial polarization around the church's focus being "on success," on the one hand and "on faithfulness," on the other. Even though you could say I bought into the "faithfulness" end of that spectrum, there still needed to be a strong organization, institution, in place in order for the "faithfulness" to take place. And so, "success" and its markers of funding and attendance at religious activities (the key one being worship services), never could be taken out of the picture and always fought for primacy.

For likely the first 20 years or so of my professional work, I worked from the model of working to improve the church program so that people would be interested enough in it to attend activities, be they worship, education, or service.

Then, realizing no matter how "bright and shiny the toy" that people were simply not interested in playing church anymore, I shifted to lead the congregation to serve in the community as the expression of their faith, attempting to provide orientation and training to members to invite others in the community that they were serving to come and join the church. Even though mainline church members know and believe that getting others to join the church, become members, is key to the institution's work, it's been traditionally very difficult getting folks to do the inviting and marketing needed to grow the membership. Then, shifting from a "come and see" mentality that does focus on inviting (however little inviting was done) to a "go and be" mentality that focuses on serving in the community (with hopes that some "church interest" would rub off on folks and they would join the church) made it perhaps even more challenging to grow membership (note too, this shift in mentality is difficult for church members who have only known church as an institution they know and love and needs membership growth to sustain it).

About 30 years or so ago it became popular in church to begin to describe the purpose of church as growing and developing disciples rather than recruiting members. The focus became "discipleship" rather than "membership."15

As helpful and on target in being a descriptive of what a relationship with Jesus looks like, there was still a missing of the mark for the reasons I delineated in the first chapter above: a religious consciousness prevails, a consciousness where God is the Supernatural Being to Explain the Unexplainable and the "Deus Ex Machina" to Solve the Unsolvable. In other words, the "discipleship approach," still very popular today, while an improvement over the "membership approach," still had the overall objective of creating a community (or, more mechanically speaking, building an institution) that not only still has the tendency to operate as if it is "one piece of the pie" – remember The Wholeness Wheel described earlier – but also to believe and

---

15 Rouse, Richard, *Go Make Disciples: An Invitation to Baptismal Living: A Handbook to the Catechumenate*, (Minneapolis, MN: Augsburg Fortress, 2012)

follow a God who demands that we suspend human autonomy and responsibility.

Church renewal, then, over these past few decades, has been about changing styles and methods. Much if not most of "renewal" has been about worship music, liturgy and worship service components' content.

Believe it or not, and I have a hard time believing it but it's still true, there are many in the current church who are still debating and arguing over whether it is "contemporary" or even "indigenous" worship rather than "traditional" worship that will interest if not attract the unchurched and the de-churched. Church renewal has been about changing formats of a religious consciousness rather than about changing to a world-come-of-age consciousness where at the core, all is grace because of God, displayed, if you will, in Jesus Christ and God is not here to help us out in our projects of success, safety and security but, to put it bluntly if not exclusively, we are here to help God out in God's project of healing and blessing the whole of creation, earth and humanity.

Church renewal has been about upgrading and improving the look and feel of church, but the core theology, ecclesiology and social ethic have not changed. We have a church today that is trying to renew its look but is empty at its core.

People who are not a part of the church today have little stomach and less time for debates over church styles and methods.

It seems to me that people who are not a part of the church today do want to engage what is real about God and what is real about a community who believes in God that serves the world. A church with a religious consciousness and religious Christianity will not be able to engage those people that have walked away from church or even have walked away from God. What we need is a world-come-of-age consciousness and a religion-less Christianity.

5

What Church Renewal Looks Like in a Religion-less Christianity

Many years back I worked up a mission development plan for starting a new congregation in our Florida-Bahamas Synod.16 I shared it with some Synod leaders at the time but it never got much traction and a big part of that was that it didn't have a good sustainable financial plan as part of the business plan. That being said, its core theological grounding was a theology of the cross, a theology identified as such by Martin Luther in 1518 (500 years ago this year!) in what we now call "The Heidelberg Disputation."

---

16 "167," is what I called the plan and the congregation-to-be: for the number of hours in a given week that are not devoted to the traditional one hour of the week of worship that too often alone singularly define how people think of being church. We need church to be what a person is, totally, not what a person attends, partially, and we need a way to have congregations live that out and not hold it as an idealistic concept.

I say this here, without being able because of time and the need for brevity (and because others have done this explaining well enough and better than I can[17]) to describe or unpack this understanding of cross and resurrection, because it is mission development, how to do church today, renew church today in relation to religion-less Christianity, that is our topic, and I believed years ago, and still believe today, the theology of the cross is crucial (no pun intended) to getting church development right. As I was working through more reflections on Bonhoeffer's Religion-less Christianity I was excited to see that Larry Rasmussen, in his *Dietrich Bonhoeffer's Significance for North Americans*, the book I have spent a lot of time reading and re-reading while on Sabbatical, dedicates a full chapter on "An Ethic of the Cross."

---

[17] Forde, Gerhard O., *On Being a Theologian of the Cross: Reflections on Luther's Heidelberg Disputation, 1518*, (Grand Rapids MI: Eerdmans Publishing Company)

I'm working it out in my mind these days just how the theological grounding of an ethic of the cross, a living out of Luther's Theology of the Cross, can be and is in full conversation with a world-come-of-age consciousness that sees God as superfluous for explaining reality and aiding humanity (remember our two key descriptives above regarding the world-come-of-age consciousness). And I want to get to a point where I can describe what church can be and do (ecclesiology and ethic) based on an understanding of God (theology) not as The Great Explanation or the Great Helper but as the suffering, dying and living one who embraces all reality.

To set out some foundational thinking in this regard, and to take advantage of his excellent summation of conclusions of what an ethic of the theology of the cross looks like that can help us describe a church with a world-come-of-age consciousness, I share with you below an extensive piece from Rasmussen.[18]

---

[18] Rasmussen, Larry and Bethge, Renate, *Dietrich Bonhoeffer: His Significance for North Americans* (Eugene, Oregon: Wipf and Stock Publishers, 2016), 144-145.

"-For historical reasons the ethics of the theology of the cross (theologia crucis) have been badly underdeveloped.
Dietrich Bonhoeffer is an improvement upon Martin Luther, but further changes are needed.
-The theology of the cross radically alters some common notions of 'ethics.' Ethics does not address the movement from vice to virtue but from vice and virtue combined to the 'realization of reality' (Bonhoeffer).
-This means that the point of departure for Christian ethics is not an analysis of the human condition, or patterns of character and conduct in the world, or our knowledge of good and evil, whether innate or acquired. The point of departure is the new creation in Jesus Christ as Lord.
-Christian faith means living in and with the 'old aeon' on the terms of the 'new.' This is the source of the unrelenting tension in the relationship of Christ and culture. For us neither the formulation of that relationship by Ernst Troeltsch nor its elaboration by H. Richard Niebuhr is the most helpful.
-The 'imitation of Christ' is the most promising and most underdeveloped dimension of the theology of the cross. It has been frustrated by continued Constantinian assumptions on the part of those who have held a theology of the cross. Bonhoeffer's own struggle here is significant for us.
-A Christology that is not simultaneously a social ethic is not a biblical Christology.
-An ecclesiology that is not simultaneously a social ethic is not a biblical ecclesiology.
-Against the North American theology of glory (theologia gloriae) of bourgeois optimism and its religion of legitimation and human 'coping,' the theology of the cross (theologia crucis) understands Christ existing as community as the church's societal vocation; and the way of the cross, especially messianic suffering, is the strong line (cantus firmus) in a celebration of the full range of human experience"

A renewed church today needs first a renewed theology.

God is revealed and known in the suffering and death of Jesus of Nazareth. What this means is that God is revealed and known in the humanity of humanity. The way of God that we are invited to know and live is trusting God while in our total humanity and living for God in our total humanity. A life of faith is trusting God as we go and living for God, the blessing and healing of the world, in what we do.

We have many questions and things to explain, but God is not the Explainer or the Explanation. We have many challenges and problems to solve, but God is not the Solver or the Solution.

A Christian, then, lives in God and for God without God. In God: radical reliance. For God: radical obedience. Without God: we know that God is not here to bail us out and in fact it is in the cry of dereliction (Jesus: "My God, my God, why have you forsaken me!?") that we know this most clearly.

The church today needs a renewed ecclesiology.

Church, the people called by God to live in God and live out the mission of God (the blessing and healing of the world), does not center its life in worship of God nor in service to others. The church centers its life in Jesus Christ.

Because today's church needs to change course from a religious consciousness to a world-come-of-age consciousness, and because the forms and methods of church today are declining and closing up shop, church needs to take on a different form and method.

In his prison time Bonhoeffer began developing more his thinking on "religion-less Christianity" and "unconscious Christianity" and wrote to his friend Eberhard Bethge an "Outline for a Book." It was a book he did not get to write and we are left tantalizingly close to having a full look at Bonhoeffer's thinking on how to be a Christian in a world-come-of-age. But we do have the "outline" (and of course other specific writings, mostly in his letters and papers from prison).

To help in our thinking of what church could look like in a world-come-of-age I'll share here a brief part of his "conclusions" from the "outline":

> *"The church is church only when it is there for others. As a first step it must give away all its property to those in need. The clergy must live solely on the freewill offerings of the congregations and perhaps be engaged in some secular vocation. The church must participate in the worldly tasks of life in the community – not dominating but helping and serving. It must tell people in every calling what a life with Christ is, what it means "to be there for others."*

In another writing, this one again from prison but an essay or sermon entitled "Thoughts on the Day of Baptism of D.W.R. May 1944" Bonhoeffer shares what I think is a helpful description of the fundamental dynamics of church life:

> *"Our church has been fighting during these years only for its self-preservation, as if that were an end in itself. It has become incapable of bringing the word of reconciliation and redemption to humankind and to the world.*
> *So the words we used before must lose their power, be silenced, and <u>we can be Christians today in only two ways, through prayer and in doing justice among human</u> beings. All Christian thinking, talking, and organizing must be born anew, out of that prayer and action. By the time you grow up, the form of the church will have changed considerably.*
>
> *It is still being melted and remolded, and every attempt to help it develop prematurely into a powerful organization again will only delay its conversion and purification.*

It is not for us to predict the day – but the day will come - when people will once more be called to speak the word of God in such a way that the world is changed and renewed."19

"Prayer and Action" could be the simple and straightforward description we need. Prayer here meaning all that we can do to be in conversation with the life, death and resurrection of Jesus.

Again, Bonhoeffer:

"What we imagine a God could and should do – the God of Jesus Christ has nothing to do with all that. We must immerse ourselves again and again, for a long time and quite calmly, in Jesus' life, his sayings, actions, suffering and dying in order to recognize what God promises and fulfills."20

The church doesn't need property in order to be in conversation with Jesus. Yes, to gather, for either worship, socializing or teaching/learning, we need a place to gather. But the core of life together is prayer and action, so owning and maintaining property as an organization is not necessary.

---

19 De Gruchy, John, English Edition Editor, *Dietrich Bonhoeffer Letters and Papers from Prison*, Dietrich Bonhoeffer Works Volume 8 (Minneapolis, MN: Fortress Press, 2010), 389-390.
20 De Gruchy, John, English Edition Editor, *Dietrich Bonhoeffer Letters and Papers from Prison*, Dietrich Bonhoeffer Works Volume 8 (Minneapolis, MN: Fortress Press, 2010), 514-515.

As tough as this is for us to see, it's going to be important for us to realize and do so that the resources of selling existing property can be used to fuel the new mission communities and so that the new mission communities will not be tempted to be drawn back into being a community that exists to support the infrastructure of the institution.

As church we need theologians and pastors so that the gospel is caught and taught in the mission communities, but there need not be a pastor for every Prayer and Action community. Though this is good news for a church where now the number of pastors trained and deployed has dropped precipitously, the training of our pastors needs to be focused not only on theological and spiritual formation (so that Gospel can be done in the communities they serve) but also on teaching skills and community building and community organizing skills (it is and will not be easy developing church communities, mission communities, that own no property. The Prayer and Action will be what holds the community together, not the brick and mortar and place to gather).

I don't mean to say here that we as church today need to start selling off properties that are and can be supported and sustained. The focus should not be on the property issues we have. The focus needs to be on the forming of "Prayer and Action" communities with or without properties.

Then, as now and will be more and more, when we have properties to sell, we need not be anxious because the selling doesn't mean the end of the mission communities.

Larry Rasmussen has a helpful synopsis and analysis of Bonhoeffer's thinking on ecclesiology and ethics, prayer and action, to help us in this quest for renewal and how a religion-less Christianity can be the way forward in renewal. In referring to the passage from the "Thoughts on Baptism" Bonhoeffer piece I shared above, most specifically on the reference to "prayer and action," Rasmussen writes:

"If we set these few lines within Bonhoeffer's own practice, they become suggestive for the rhythm of Christian living in a world come of age. In fact, they reflect a lively dialectic Bonhoeffer lived out in the church struggle of the 1930's and the resistance movement of the late 1930's and early 1940's.

What are the poles of the dialectic? Naming the first is easy, because Bonhoeffer does so, taking the early Christian community's name: the hidden, or arcane, discipline. Naming the second is not as easy because Bonhoeffer does not provide the term. It concerns "doing justice among men," or, viewed in its theological dimension, with participation 'in the sufferings of God in the secular life.' For lack of a better term, we shall call it "costly worldly solidarity."[21]

Rasmussen goes on to describe both an "Arcane Discipline" and a "Costly Worldly Solidarity" as key for the dynamics of renewal.[22] Some characteristics I'll glean from Rasmussen's work:

<u>Arcane Discipline</u>

-church of the future as low-profile order in the world as the world come of age

- "arcane" or "hidden" disciplines means what the discipleship community does to keep itself being the church in the world come of age: prayer, bible, worship, spiritual practices

---

[21] Rasmussen, Larry and Bethge, Renate, *Dietrich Bonhoeffer: His Significance for North Americans* (Eugene, Oregon: Wipf and Stock Publishers, 2016), 68.

[22] Rasmussen, Larry and Bethge, Renate, *Dietrich Bonhoeffer: His Significance for North Americans* (Eugene, Oregon: Wipf and Stock Publishers, 2016), 68-69.

- "…worship is not for everyone. It is for small groups of committed Christians who comprise an intense community on the basis of their intense loyalty to Christ."

- "if Bonhoeffer were to have his way, the church would begin by giving up its property for the sake of the needy, would be devout in its practice of disciplines, and demanding in its stipulations for participation. It would be a poor and apparently powerless church that would dispense costly grace, rather than a rich and privileged church that offers cheap grace."

-all biblical material and all theological categories need to be approached from a non-religious interpretation

Costly Worldly Solidarity

-Christians serving others and creation in the world without pretense

-doing justice work in secular ways in the public arena

- "it is costly solidarity as participation in the sufferings of God in the secular life"

It seems to me that "Prayer and Action" are not only helpful indentifiers for renewal because they are short and memorable but also because in their fullness they are comprehensive in describing the heartbeat of the disciple's life.

6

Conclusion

What we have in Dietrich Bonhoeffer's work on "religion-less Christianity" is an opening to be able to form a working theology for mission today. It is going to take some work and some courage by leaders and disciples to engage this opening and engage the changing methods of doing mission in our world that wants less and less to do with church.

Certainly I have not provided answers for what we will look like in doing mission with a "religion-less Christianity, but I hope I have described enough about what a "religion-less Christianity" is and could be, based on what I have been learning from Bonhoeffer and others, in order to spur on church renewal that will be faithful to the gospel and real for today's world.

Perhaps to highlight not only that we have a lot of figuring to do and to lean on the fact that many times good questions more that good answers provide more possibility for growth, I conclude with some questions below that may help drive us forward in faith and mission.

Regarding "Prayer" and Renewal:

-what opportunities for teaching the life, sayings, death and resurrection of Jesus are going on week by week in our church communities?

-what opportunities for small groups to form and be communities of prayer and action?

-How can corporate worship, with all its necessary planning and implementing, be less of a focus for the church today so that engagement of Scripture and engagement of building friendship and relationships might flourish more?

Regarding "Costly Worldly Solidarity" and Renewal

-how does the church teach that vocation, calling from God, is done by serving *as* the church in family, community and workplace not serving *in* the church in congregational life support? In other words, what teaching and support is done so that in the 3 key areas of vocation (family, community, workplace) disciples are best equipped to serve God in the world (in addition to the traditional calling/vocation that most people associate with being a part of church: serving the congregation by volunteering to support the program and property)

-where are the opportunities for church disciples to serve together in the community this week?

7

Appendix: Part One
Journal Jottings on Religion-less Christianity
December 2017 – July 2018

Journal December 22, 2017

What is Religion-less Christianity?

How can I describe for your Dietrich Bonhoeffer's "religion-less Christianity?"

It is saying that God, in Jesus, and therefore always even without Jesus, is not the "God of the gaps," here to fill our need where we need or our lack of information when we are lacking. God is not a power or being that stands ready at our beck and call to help us achieve and perfect the power to which we aspire.

God does not stand at the periphery of our center in order to expand or enhance our place or influence. God, rather, is the center of all existence and we live within this being. Our humanity is not aided by divinity, but rather is divinity, but not by an elevation of humanity to divinity, and, perhaps, not even by a deflation of divinity to humanity (the New Testament, e. g. Philippians 2, does describe this descending), but rather by a revelation that humanity in all its dearth and dust, is where the divine always has lived and will only live for the sake of, or as the expression of, the only thing that God (divinity) is which is this: self-giving love.

I am thinking right now of a couple of related descriptions of all this:

1. Luther's statement of God only being found in suffering and death (note the "only")
2. My illustration of salvation where the drowning victim is met by the arriving "life-guard" who only saves by promising to die with the drowning victim and then does just that.

Journal April 7, 2018

Religion-less Christianity – God at the Center

"how do we talk about God.... the difference between the penultimate and the ultimate have new significance? Letters and Papers from Prison (LPP), pp. 364-365

This April 22, 1944 letter is, I believe, as I read through LPP, Dietrich Bonhoeffer's (DB) first more detailed exploration of Religion-less Christianity.

Within this section of letter:

"Christ would then no longer be the inject of religion, but something else entirely, truly Lord of the world. But what does that mean? In a religion-less situation, what do ritual and prayer mean?"

It is hard for us, perhaps naturally so, in the sense of sinfully so, in the sense of we cannot not think of ourselves at the center or allow God to be at the center instead of on the periphery.

To allow God, thinking of "the Wholeness Wheel" here, to be the entire wheel, the entire "pie," instead of a spoke in the wheel or a piece of the pie. But that is what a RC is. It is Christ as all there is. It is Christ as subject who acts on us and not object on whom we act.

I've often illustrated the place of cultus and prayer, spiritual practices, with the time of Haught's International Justice Ministry and how the attorneys on staff there that do the work of advocacy and action against human trafficking, must stop 2 times a day for prayer and bible reading simply because they cannot do the life and work of justice, in and for Christ, without God, without Christ. Prayer and devotions (DB's "arcane discipline") is here not a last resort, a going to God when all else fails, a turning to an aspect of reality that can assist the true reality or whole reality. It is rather a first resort, a going to God because God is all there is, because god is where we live.

What would become of our faith if we took away Sunday worship?

What if the church, the "called out ones," stopped producing worship services on Sunday mornings?

To imagine this brings us face to face with the vacuousness of our faith and the nature of religion.

Journal April 17, 2018

Religion-less Christianity and Random Disasters

On NPR *On-Point* show tonight, seismologist with new book, "The Big Ones," spoke well on random disasters and how scientifically we know how, earthquakes, for example, are random acts of nature, that destroy, but humans, with our penchant for order and meaning, cast blame, and historically have chosen one way to do that in religion: the gods are capricious (mythologies), or, in Judaism/Christianity, God is good (covenant) but we must have disobeyed (note: brain/thinking of homosapiens uses order/meaning to create safety/security whereas other animals use other mechanisms, self-defense/safety, to address random dangers and disaster).

All this relates to Religion-less Christianity: we are "come of age" by knowing God is not necessary to explain phenomenon, e.g. disasters, but we are uncomfortable in knowing what religion is or how to be a follower of God without this understanding of God as being the "stop-gap." Bonhoeffer, I believe is arguing that Christianity never was a "religion as stop-gap" and we, in our time of figuring what Christ means today, what it means to be a Christian today, are seeing this.

We are seeing, and need to see, how to talk of God, and follow God, while God is all and not a part of life, where religion is not a dimension of life to apply to our circumstances but rather is everything, encompassing everything, our total humanity, not a Shaman to make us divine or separate us from humanity (with its random disasters).

While the religious see pushing God out of our conversation of natural life (including randomness) as the death of spirituality and

God, those "born again" (to use a phrase!) see it very differently: as a Religion-less Christianity, as an invigorating exploration of the existence and relevance of God.

Not surprisingly, the way forward is to march backward to the actual life and death and resurrection of Jesus, and to have theology be what it is: a talking about history, not history about a talking. Bible is not a history about God, but a God about history. It is not a history about theology, but a theology about history. For example, the assertion/subversion rhythm of grace and judgement, non-violence and violence, in Scripture, is not some unified or uniform whole that defines or speaks for God or as God, a "history" about theology, but rather human writers grappling with two approaches to conflict and creation, a "theology about history," where we now need to figure out and determine which actually is the approach we will take, the lifestyle and value system we will live, the understanding of God we will apply to history…….

Journal May 4, 2018

On Religion-less Christianity and Being Made New

Yesterday at the National Day of Prayer Celebration about 100 folks gathered at Annie Donnelly Park in downtown Mt. Dora and lots of prayers were prayed. One prayer caught my heart as the leader prayed thanks for creation and for us as being creation too, of God, but then also he went on to say, "but thankyou O God, for being made a new creation in Christ Jesus." He's correct, of course, and spot on biblically: "so if anyone is in Christ Jesus there is a new creation, everything old has passed away." But this is precisely where we turn the wrong corner, usually, with the faith. This transformation that takes place. What is it? What changes? How is the creature new because of Christ Jesus? Bonhoeffer writes July 18, 1944 to Eberhard Bethge (in one of the letters most spiced with "religion-less" thinking): "Being a Christian does not mean being religious in a certain way, making oneself into something or other (a sinner, penitent, or saint) according to some method or other. Instead it means being human, not a certain type of human being, but the human being Christ creates in us" (note: see *Life Together*, the week of January 25, 2018).

The wrong turn we take with "new creation" is thinking that in Christ we are now different than human if not more than human. The "human being" that Christ creates in us is the one that being born in flesh and blood actually is.

"Born again," to use a phrase, is not to get beyond, now our skin, but to be made comfortable in the only thing I have: my own skin. Our "problem," if that is what we can call it, is that we don't like who and what we are: mortal skin and bones. Human. We cannot allow ourselves to be here and gone, to not be the center of things, to not exist. How could someone else be the center, be the thing, be the immortal?

What Christ does is knock us off the high horse of pride and bring us down to our humanity as well as lift us up from the dregs of despair and haul us up to our humanity.

How is this all "religion-less Christianity"? Religion is a spiritual construction project we initiate, manage and complete. Christianity is a human life experience we receive and live within. Religion says a new creation is no longer creation. Christianity says a new creation is only and ever will be creation.

Journal July 2, 2018

On the Cross, Religion, Social Ethic

The Cross cannot be used, it cannot be interpreted, it cannot be understood. Even to say "it can only be experienced" is an appropriation and a step into a religion.

To say "Crux Sola Est Nostra Theologia" (The Cross Alone is our Theology), Luther's landmark description from The Heidelberg Disputation of 1518, it must be understood how "theologia gloria" (theology of glory) is its opposite and must be understood as a description of life and death and not a prescription for health and well-being.

I am understanding in these days that the social ethic of the Crux Sola Est Nostra Theologia (C-SENT = Cross Sent!) still needs to be written. Larry Rasmussen is correct (in *Dietrich Bonhoeffer: His Significance for North Americans*) in saying the theology of the cross too easily and readily deflates and conflates into another theology of glory.

C-SENT insists that hope only is found in love embracing death. It's like my image of salvation for a drowning person: not a rescue to shore but an embrace by the lifeguard in the water and the rescuer, the lifeguard, and the rescued, the drowning person, drown together.

Journal July 6, 2018

On Church Renewal

Attempts at church renewal today are falling flat not because of inadequate or poor programming or marketing, although there is plenty of that. The flight from religion is about something deep and fundamental, not surface and technical.

The fight to bring people back to church life, to say nothing of back to God, does not recognize the major shift that has been taking place for the past century, and the attempts to revitalize that have been going on are like providing a new coat of paint on a decaying structure rather than constructing a new building.

Dietrich Bonhoeffer called the shift that is upon us a move from a religious consciousness to a world-come-of-age consciousness.

It is vital that as Christians who find vitality and meaning in the story of Jesus, and who want to share this story as our way of contributing to the witness to (God's) love if not also the healing of the world, live and tell this story with the honesty and integrity in this post-religious era in which we live (and one that, I would argue, Jesus inaugurated but the church lost). Church renewal efforts today are trying to fix up the church so that it can continue to be religious. It's no wonder those efforts are falling flat when we no longer live in a religious consciousness as a society. Let's take some time to define religious consciousness and world-come-of-age consciousness before we go any further.

Journal July 9, 2018

Jesus Asks the Questions: (Preaching) Jesus, The Four Questions and the World-Come-Of-Age Consciousness

I saw a sermon on You-Tube yesterday from one of the pastors in our Evangelical Lutheran Church in America and as I watched I worked to track it to its core message.

Well done delivery, but I fear a fairly common psychologizing of the story of Jesus. I listen, when I do get a chance to hear a sermon, for how "gospel of Jesus" and "grace" and other all too familiar terms are used and I see they are left unpacked and undefined. Or, more to the point, left defined as answers of acceptance and encouragements to all our pathologies, with a bit of urging to change our behaviors thrown in as a nod at transformation.

We all do need hope, to be sure. And we are all looking for a place of grace. But that hope that comes from grace is counterfeited when Jesus speaks into our weaknesses instead of our strengths, when Jesus is a religion, a rescue from our weakness instead of a world-come-of-age presence, a director to our strengths.

I have been operating now, theologically, for years, around the base-line questions that are four-fold: Who Am I? Where Do I Belong? What is the Meaning of My Life, and What Will Become of Me? I still think these are fundamental and existential and global, but a Religion-less Christianity engages them differently than I have been thinking. I can, in a world-come-of-age consciousness, answer all of those questions. In other words, I can answer those questions without turning to the divine or calling upon God.

In fact, I do answer those questions daily with my own devices and machinations.

For example, I am an American, I belong to the International Coach Federation and the Cross-Creek Neighborhood Association, my purpose is taking care of my family and my destiny is unknown. Religion tries to tell me those are the wrong answers. As I have framed it in the past, I have answered each with "Jesus Christ," and found that not only to be true in that it flattens all personal constructions but also troubling because that answer is virtually unexplainable or untranslatable and opaque, a mysterious, spiritual language to any person not familiar with religious language or spirituality. It ends up being, simply saying "Jesus Christ," although true enough even in a world-come-of-age consciousness, a religious answer to a human question.

What I am seeing now is that the world-come-of-age consciousness forces, nay allows, me to let Jesus be who he actually is: the one who asks the questions rather than answers them!

Jesus is not the answer to our four questions, he is the one who asks them, or more correctly, he can be the one who asks them.

In other words, many people can ask them, and do, but if Jesus asks them, they come from one with a specific and particular life and death and resurrection content, place and perspective.

I'm thinking of how Dietrich Bonhoeffer speaks of now needing to pay close attention to the teaching, life, actions, death and resurrection of Jesus. We need to track Jesus, not our religious appropriation of him.

So, if he asks us the four questions, rather than someone else asking us the four questions, the point of departure from exploration has a specific content. The launch pad is constructed of materials with a particular consistency and substance. Call this material self-giving love.

All this requires an on-going definition of Jesus. An attention to him. And so, a new kind of reading of the Gospels, and the entire New Testament and Hebrew Scriptures. One that I have acquiring and using for some time, years, and which makes me constantly suspicious of traditional interpretations and explanations. Jesus is not the answer. He is the question. And it's comforting as well as challenging to have the question come from him.

Journal July 10, 2018

Reading Mark 14 and Being Church from a World-Come-Of-Age Consciousness

In Mark 14 desertion permeates the story. V. 27: "you will all become deserters." V. 29 "even though all will become deserters I will not."

What does a community today do with a story like this? Why and how have we created such a cultus, worship, around such a story (not just Mark 14, but the whole Jesus story)?

Dietrich Bonhoeffer speaks of the only thing necessary (if not also possible given the actual facts of the Christian story) are Prayer and Action. But so much of the church's energy and focus is on worship, albeit a form of Prayer, around and from a religious consciousness.

Because of this focus on worship activities the Action is therefore and thereby muffled if not muted if not never delivered. How might chapter 14 of Mark be a call to not desert the cause even as we do desert the cause? But be careful of how we define "the cause," that it not be or become our 21st century moral or cultural agenda.

Just what is the cause of Jesus? And how do I live it?

Journal July 19, 2018

On Reading the Bible from a World-Come-Of-Age Consciousness and Learning How to Die So That We Might Actually Live.

Reading, today, randomly, Obadiah and Amos 9. So much in the divine narrative concerning land and possession. I do not read Scripture anymore from a perspective of the divine as the subject doing the speaking to the human as the object doing the listening. Well, yes, but only as determined such by faith, not de facto by fact. I rather have the hermeneutic suspicion and take this perspective: the human as subject doing the speaking and the diving as the object doing the listening. The human writers have hopes, fears, aspirations and desperations and they express them fully and recruit God to their concern and cause. When does a word from God break through? It is hard to discern. Any talk of destruction is suspect. Even from someone like Amos who has distributive justice and not retributive justice on his mind. Is it simply the human penchant for revenge that drives the deflation into retribution?

The problem, of course, with non-violent resistance is that you are more likely to be killed, and that, it seems, is the end of that. But there are reverberations and remembrances among the living that do emerge. Only some become shining stars, like Martin Luther King, Jr. and Ghandi. But there must be thousands.

But even that being said, what does it matter, this being remembered or this life continuing in any manner by those still living? Why isn't it simply enough to have lived and died? And then in death to be forgotten. Why isn't that enough? The life and death of Jesus points to this. Recognize beauty, live justly, die ignominiously and possibly even, more likely actually, inconsequentially. One only learns how to live when one learns how to die.

8

Appendix: Part Two
Life Together E-Letter Postings
January – May 2018

Introduction to the Weekly E-letter *Life Together* and the Topic of Bonhoeffer's Religion-less Christianity

I write a weekly e-letter called *Life Together* for my congregation, St. Philip Lutheran Church, Mt. Dora, Florida. In 2018 I decided, because it is the year of my sabbatical, I would simply dedicate the *Life Together* weekly postings to my sabbatical's "Reflection" component, Dietrich Bonhoeffer's "religion-less Christianity." The weekly postings are not meant to be systematic or organized in a way that they would necessarily build on each other or create a sequence of thought. They are weekly musings and thinking on "religion-less Christianity" that are posted as stand-alones.

You may notice too that there are breaks in the weekly schedule at times. Simply put, there were weeks when Life Together did not get written!

A bit more background:

When Dietrich Bonhoeffer, German Lutheran Pastor and Teaching Theologian, was imprisoned in 1943 by the Nazi Regime for anti-government (Nazi) activity and before he was executed in April 1945 under personal order of Hitler himself after never being released from prison, he wrote letters, essays, poems, and narratives both fiction and non-fiction. Toward the end of his imprisonment he wrote an outline to a book he never got to write. And in the last year of his imprisonment, and thus too his life, and what looked like to be what would be the focus of this unpublished book, he was writing of this thing called a "religion-less Christianity." We never got the book. We never got the complete thinking of Bonhoeffer on the subject, but we got good thinking, writing, and ruminations to capture our imagination and call us to engage the faith in what Bonhoeffer called "a world come of age."

2018 is my sabbatical and the congregation's renewal year and the bulk of my sabbatical time is June – August. In the sabbatical there are four foci: reflection, recreation, relationships, restoration. The "reflection" portion is on Bonhoeffer's "religion-less Christianity."

Life Together the First week of 2018

Let's get started.

How can I describe for you Dietrich Bonhoeffer (DB)'s "religion-less" Christianity?

"It is saying that God, in Jesus, and therefore always even without Jesus, is not the "God of the gaps," here to fill our need where we need or our lack of information when we are lacking. God is not a power or being that stands ready at our beckon call to help us achieve and perfect the power and position to which we aspire. God does not stand at the periphery of our center in order to expand or enhance our place or influence. God, rather, is the center of all existence and we live within this being.

Our humanity is not aided by divinity, but rather is divinity, but not as an elevation of humanity to divinity, and (perhaps) not as a deflation of divinity (c.f. the New Testament, e.g. Philippians 2 describing the decent of God to earth in Jesus), but rather by a revelation that humanity in all of its dearth and dust, is where the divine always has dwelt and will only dwell for the sake of or as the expression of the only thing that God (divinity) is: self-giving love. I am thinking right now of a couple of related descriptions of all of this: 1) Martin Luther's statement that God is only found in suffering and death (note the word "only") 2) an illustration of salvation I have conjured up and used many times that positions a drowning person being met by an arriving "life guard" who only saves by promising to die along with the drowning person and then does just that."

Okay, here's an interesting thing that as I think of it sheds some light not only on how I will be sharing my thoughts in 2018 on religion-less Christianity in Life Together but also expresses how we actually received DB's direct address on this subject: the section above in quotes is something I wrote in my daily journal on December 22 and as I went back to it to share here I was typing along and realized when I got to the end it was really an incomplete essay, not a full or well-rounded exposition, and that more needed to be said and that the thoughts needed to be organized (not to say also vetted!). DB's *Letters and Papers in Prison*, where we get his direct address on religion-less Christianity (let's call it RC), were just that: letters and papers. My thoughts in Life Together on RC will be that too. Not fully thought out, not fully organized, not fully edited, just shared. And to give you an idea of how unvarnished what that sharing will be, here's what I wrote in my journal on Dec. 22 just after I finished the above and as I was typing the above out now found abruptly disturbing because what I wrote begged for more description/explanation: "cleaned house, did laundry, got haircut, did some home finance."

I went from noting DB's RC to chronicling my chores. Ah, yes. And such is the way we live our life.

So, there you have it for now. Some initial ramblings on DB's RC and my engagement of it and sharing with you. Again, now in 2018, I'll be using Life Together to just keep opening up this RC as much as possible. At least that's the way if feels right now.

In Life Together with You,

Pastor Johan

Life Together the week of January 7 2018

"'Could you not stay awake with me one hour?' Jesus asks us in Gethsemane. That is the opposite of everything a religious person expects from God. The human being is called upon to share in God's suffering at the hands of a godless world.

Thus we must really live in that godless world and not try to cover up or transfigure its godlessness with religion.

Our lives must be 'worldly,' so that we can share precisely so in God's suffering: our lives are allowed to be 'worldly,' that is, we are delivered from false religious obligations and inhibitions. Being a Christian does not mean being religious in a certain way, making oneself into something or other (a sinner, penitent, or saint) according to some method or other. Instead it means being human, not a certain type of human being, but the human being Christ creates in us. It is not a religious act that makes someone a Christian, but rather sharing in God's suffering in the worldly life. That is "metanoia," not thinking first of one's owns needs, questions, sins, and fears but allowing oneself to be pulled into walking the path that Jesus walks, into the messianic event, in which Isaiah 53 is now being fulfilled"

(Dietrich Bonhoeffer (DB) in a portion of the letter to friend Eberhard Bethge, from prison, July 18, 1944, *Letters and Papers from Prison*, Dietrich Bonhoeffer Works, Volume 8, p. 480)

How can it not be a "religious act" but "sharing in God's suffering in the worldly life" when the "sharing" is actually an act, something we do? To get this we have to go to the root of the word "suffer," which is a letting be, an allowing of something to happen (e.g. "suffer the little children to come to me" = let the children come to me). We have to go to "suffering" as something that happens to us when we let the world and God happen to us. At the root of our human life (note: not religious life) is a suffering of God: we suffer the fact that there is pain and hurt in the world, and in our lives, and God seems (is?!) absent! (Jesus on cross: "My God, my God, why have you abandoned me!?"). Then DB says though we are not religious, but human, there is a humanity that "Christ creates." What is that? That sounds religious again! If Christ creates something in us doesn't that make us religious? No, it makes us human with hope instead of despair.

In Life Together with you,

Pastor Johan

Life Together the week of January 14 2018

"What we imagine of God could and should do – the God of Jesus Christ has nothing to do with all that." (Dietrich Bonhoeffer (DB) in a portion of the letter to friend Eberhard Bethge, from prison, August 21, 1944, *Letters and Papers from Prison*, Dietrich Bonhoeffer Works, Volume 8, p. 515)

What we imagine God would or could do is to be omnipotent, omniscient, omnipresent, "omni-holy," and "omni-just." We bring this picture of God as defined by attributes to the table of life because of who we are in our need for identity, community, meaning and destiny. God, we surmise, should deliver to us what we want and when we need it and should do so at our call, not God's call.

What we find in Jesus is the utter empty and vacuous nature of all this definition of God. I

In his life he only lives with the least, last, lost, little and the dead.

In his death he is not vindicated but simply brutally executed.

In his resurrection he is vindicated, but what is vindicated is the suffering of God (the passive resignation of living at the hand of God with the passion of God for peace by justice through non-violence), not the victory of humanity.

And then, as if to make this perfectly clear, Jesus disappears never to be seen again but only to be known through the suffering (faith) of never seeing and only hearing (faith…. comes by hearing, Romans 10).

In Life Together with you,

Pastor Johan

Life Together the week of January 21 2018

"By contrast, he [Bonhoeffer] wanted to speak of God at the center of life and address men and women in their strength, that is, their maturity and autonomy as responsible human beings" (John W. de Gruchy, Editor, Dietrich Bonhoeffer Works, Vol. 8, Letters and Papers from Prison)

God is not the answer to life's questions but rather the question to life's answers. Or, if the not the question to the answers we wisely and astutely provide then this: the question to our questions of Who Am I, Where Do I Belong, What Is the Meaning of My Life, and What Will Become of Me. In any case, God is not the answer but rather the question that unconditional love puts to us in the face of all things. God at the center of life rather than the answer in life means, perhaps, that these questions (Who, Where, What) are what happen to us as human beings up against the ultimacies that remain beyond us, perhaps what Luther called "The Hidden God." It is the Hidden God, the God beyond us, that always remains there and, in our encounter, drives us to (easy?) answers that are sacredly fundamentalist on the one hand or secularly fundamentalist on the other hand. We divide life into sacred and secular when God is not actually in one and not the other but in both.

Actually, there is no sacred and secular. There is only a Center. God is in the center of life, all of life. Then, most profoundly, God at the center in the Christian declaration about God, that is, that God took on and is flesh and blood, humanity, means that humanity is at the center. Not a humanity without God (like religion likes to paint humanity's condition) but a humanity in God. Totally surrounded and imbued with God. It is Luther's opposite of the Hidden God, his "Revealed God," that keeps God at the center of life, humanity. God is not thus answering humanity's dilemmas or crisis, but rather questioning whether love can or will prevail in all humanity's endeavors and circumstances.

Enough of that for now.

I do have another thing to share this week that I hope might entice you to read the Bible with an open and suspicious mind and heart and encourage you to talk about what you read with others and learn about what you read. It comes from my devotions and journal this week. I'll call it "Not My Prayer – Psalm 18"

Not My Prayer – Psalm 18

First of all, I do not see God swooping down to save the good and well-behaved people in their distress. I see God swimming out to the drowning ones and simply telling them She is with them as they die and is dying right there with them. I see Jesus.

Secondly, if there is any swooping it isn't done with impatient anger. It is done with patient compassion. I see Jesus.

Thirdly, the arrival does not bring vengeance, but rather forgiveness. I see Jesus.

Lastly, I don't see God siding with one tribe to subjugate or eliminate another. I see God leveling the field of class and culture so that all experience and participate in God's good creation. I see Jesus.

John Dominic Crossan writes: *"When the academy reconstructs the historical Jesus, is he non-violent or violent? Also, when the* church confesses the evangelical Christ, is he non-violent or violent?

Of course the historical Jesus is profoundly and theologically significant for the biblical Christ, and Christianity, whether we like it or not, requires a theology founded and grounded on the historical Jesus. In other words, for Christians, God is revealed in Christ, but Christ is revealed in Jesus. If the norm of the Christian Bible is the biblical Christ, then the norm of the biblical Christ is the historical Jesus" (How to Read the Bible and Still be A Christian, 2015).

Psalm 18 is the prayer of a person who sees God as partisan, violent and vengeful. When we read the Bible we must be careful to see that the God represented in the accounting (stories, poems, liturgies, letters, histories, et. al.) is not always the actual mind and manner of Jesus.

And oh yes, I just remembered another aspect of the activity and character of God as Psalm 18 describes that we should see: God rewards the blameless and God's law-abiding persons and, too, the hope and goal of the God-believing person is to be blameless before God. Go ahead and read Ps. 18 again and you'll find this in there too.

And now, tell me, how that squares with Jesus, for example, with the adulterous woman, or Zacchaeus with his corrupt financial dealings, or even the close insider Peter who abandoned him (Jesus) when push came to shove. And this is to say nothing of the theological tradition built upon the historical Jesus that declares we are "saved by grace, not works of the law."

So, you see, the Bible will blow open our heart and mind and rather than have both heart and mind depressed or confused or shaped in a way harmful to you or others, it's important to not only read it and pray it but also talk about it and learn about it so that it actually works grace on you and others.

Psalm 18 is not my prayer.

It is yours?

Let's' talk about it together.

In Life Together with you,

Pastor Johan

Life Together the week of January 28 2018

Just a bit on vengeance and God…….and how we cannot legitimize vengeance by saying it's in the Bible.

"Only when one knows that the name of God may not be uttered may one sometimes speak the name of Jesus Christ.

Only when one loves life and the earth so much that with it everything seems to be lost and at its end may one believe in the resurrection of the dead and a new world. Only when on accepts the law of God as binding for oneself may one perhaps sometimes speak of grace. And only when the wrath and vengeance of God against God's enemies are allowed to stand can something of forgiveness and the love of enemies touch our hearts" Bonhoeffer, excerpt from letter to friend Eberhard Bethge, Second Sunday of Advent, 1943.

There is a sense here of the deep and abiding respect for the law of God, the demands, moral and relational, of God.

It comes from the sense of God's person being that which stands for justice and order and that all creation is the servant subject of this strength and majesty. How can one have this uber high regard for God's position and rule without using that understanding to beat down those who we think do not conform? Or this, how can we have such a deep and expansive view of God's sovereignty without being overly and obviously religious? One can easily untether law and demand from grace and have it swing as a club of death and one can easily untether grace from the law and have it be a letting off the hook without regard for reform.

But, I don't know. I wonder actually whether you can corrupt grace, the unconditional love that simply dies without demand for reform. I wonder if really there is such a thing as "cheap grace" because, truth be told, "cheap grace" isn't grace at all but rather another demand for reform. To call it "cheap," in other words, you have to be assuming that there should have been a payback, a reform, for all the grace given. "Cheap" implies that there is an opposite: "costly."

And if it is to be grace, it cannot be cheap or costly, it has to be free.

On another level, of course there is a cost to grace. But it has nothing to do with what we'd like to think: it has nothing to do with grace coming (forgiveness or a letting off the hook or a second chance or however you want to frame it) only when one has done one's best with the rigors of following the way (e.g. loving enemies). It's rather this: when one is captured by the love and passion of God for the world (and oneself) one is compelled to join in the mission.

There is no compulsion, it is merely so compelling and captivating there can be no other focus but participating with God in this love and passion for the world, in all its corruptions and frailties. In other words, you begin and continue to operate in grace for others. And then, before the day is over, and every day thereafter, the cost of doing such a thing because particularly clear: when you are graceful to others you will get burned, you will be taken advantage of, you will be let down, you will pay the price. It will cost you.

And then let's just take a look at that "wrath and vengeance of God against God's enemies" to which Bonhoeffer refers.

A Christian takes her understanding of God from the Biblical Christ and the Biblical Christ takes it's understanding of Christ from the historical Jesus. And when you look at the Jesus of Palestine you simply cannot find wrath and vengeance.
You can find wrath and vitriolic verbal thrashings and even table up turnings but you cannot wrath and vengeance.

I believe that all the "wrath" and "O, Lord, would you come down and wipe out our enemies" and all the accounts of God speaking and telling the people of Israel to wipe out whole tribes of people for the sake of religious purity.... I believe that all of that is the wishful thinking of the tribe of Israel as it was trying to make its way in a harsh environment.

I believe they wanted (their) God to act with vengeance and I believe when they took vengeance they legitimized it by theologizing it and stating in their accounting of it all that God had directed it.

It just makes sense. We are people who like to get back at those who stand against us or have hurt us.

And we legitimize this attitude and action by believing we are on the moral and doctrinal high ground and others are, well, not, and we have a right, by God (literally), to take them out. Israel in 1900 B.C.E (or so) and following was no different than we are in this regard.

But all of this runs up against and into Jesus of Nazareth and it comes to a full stop. It is killed. Vengeance and killing is killed by the one who was killed rather than take vengeance.

If this is so (and, well, it is) what are we to make of "the wrath and vengeance of God against God's enemies" to which Bonhoeffer refers? Bonhoeffer says it has to "stand" in order to see or know the forgiveness and love of enemies that transforms our hearts. Well, it can "stand," in order expose the power and liberation that comes from its opposite: forgiveness/love of enemies. But it's a misnomer. There is not vengeance that comes along with the wrath against injustice that Jesus wields. There is wrath. Jesus is fierce about his hatred for the least, last, lost, little and dead being left behind by the most first, found, big and alive. But there is no vengeance.

There is simply and forthrightly a cost to the grace given. They took his life.

And you know all the business about "vengeance is mine, says the Lord," that we find in the Bible? Do you know what that is?

That is a signal, a word from God, that vengeance is to be taken off our plate and given to God. If there is any vengeance to be taken, it's to be God, not us. And God knows God will never take it! "Vengeance is mine" is God taking it from us and burying it. But, the people of God, as I tried to describe above, ascribe to God the vengeance we take as a way to legitimize our ways. The "vengeance is mine" that takes vengeance out of the game is much like the account of Abraham and the almost human sacrifice of his son Isaac. What!? God is going to call for human sacrifice?! What kind of God does that!? The point of the story, which of course ends with God providing a way for the human sacrifice not to happen, is that the God of the people of Israel is exactly not that kind of God who requires human sacrifice! All the other gods of neighboring tribes of this nascent tribe of Israel may have gods that demand human sacrifice, but not the God of Abraham, Isaac and Jacob!

Okay, enough. Where are we here? I'm not sure, and that's the consequence of writing off the cuff. But maybe we have this: yes, there is this profound sovereignty of God that Bonhoeffer describes, and it does bring its demands on the human condition in order to make us sit up and fly right….and all the flying to be done simply in order to make the world a better place…..the place God intends……but then when push comes to shove, and it does, the sovereignty is revealed to be sacrificial and unconditional love at all costs. God simply loves us to death.

The Apostle Paul called all this "power made perfect in weakness" but we don't have time or space to say any more about that connection now.

In Life Together with you,

Pastor Johan

Life Together the week of February 11, 2018

"Furthermore, a report on the a-religiosity of college students, 'distinterested.' That must be what comes if one doesn't finally understand that 'religion' is truly superfluous."

Dietrich Bonhoeffer wrote this in his diary, June 17, 1939, while in the United States at Union Seminary, New York for a stay cut very short because he felt compelled to go back to Germany to engage the struggle with colleagues, family, and friends against Hitler's regime (*Dietrich Bonhoeffer Works*, Volume 15: Theological Education Underground 1937-1940, p. 224). He is referring to an article he read in Christian Century (56:1939) entitled "Are Students Losing Their Religion?"

In these days where we now have 20-25 % of the American population self-identifying as having no specific religious preference (the statisticians and sociologists call these folks the "Nones" because they check the box "None" when in a survey they are asked about religious preference or identification), this 1939 magazine article title question seems quaint.

But Bonhoeffers diary comment is key and points to his later thinking on "religion-less Christianity." A religious construct that takes a person away from the nitty-gritty of life, that works to somehow transcend the human and the earthliness of creation, is not the religion of following Jesus. But I am concerned that we misinterpret Bonhoeffer's "religion-less Christianity" by equating it with a spirituality that still works to transcend humanity and earth and that still works by human agency to initiate or at least further the relationship the divine. As we talk about "not being religious but yes being spiritual" as many who are

"Nones" today express their faith, it seems to me, and I may be wrong here, that although the Nones leave behind the rituals and practices of religions they do not or are not leaving behind a religious Christianity, not in Bonhoeffer's terms, when they are being spiritual but not religious.

My best take on things is that most people today don't want the strictures of the traditional religious practices and ethics (and/or don't like the menu of options available, e.g. a worship service that speaks into the 16th century and not into the 21st century or they don't like a social ethic that, for example, demonizes homosexuality, and, by the way, who does want that and who does see that as Jesus inspired!? Alas, too many) but that, in being spiritual, and casting aside the trappings of religion, both cultic and ethic, they are still very much living a religion-full Christianity. They still see the sacred and the secular as separate worlds and they still see living for God and in God as marked by specific rituals and practices. Rather than living for and in God as deeply enmeshed and engaged in life's relationships the Nones all too often simply join the Ones who do check off a religious preference in trying to set apart their life as being connected to God, the Divine, in some supernatural way instead of no way at all but remaining totally human and, therefore, de-facto, totally mortal.

So much for now. I continue to hold you all in my heart. I continue to pray that Jesus is our Way.

Take a look below for this Sunday's "Taking the Message Home" to prime the pump. I look forward to seeing you around the Table at 9:30am in Mt. Dora. And if you live elsewhere, may you find a Jesus Table where you are welcome.

In Life Together with you,

Pastor Johan

Life Together the week of February 18, 2018

"The poem 'Christians and Heathens' includes a thought that you will recognize here. 'Christians stand by God in God's own pain' – that distinguishes Christians from heathens. 'Could you not stay awake with me one hour?' Jesus asks in Gethsemane. That is the opposite of everything a religious person expects from God. The human being is called upon to share in God's suffering at the hands of a godless world.

Thus we must really live in that godless world and not try to cover up or transfigure its godlessness somehow with religion. Our lives must be 'worldly,' so that we can share precisely so in God's suffering; our lives are allowed to be 'worldly,' that is, we are delivered from false religious obligations and inhibitions. Being a Christian does not mean being religious in a certain way, making oneself into something or other (a sinner, penitent, or saint) according to some method or other.

Instead it means being human, not a certain type of human being, but the human being Christ creates in us. It is not a religious act that makes someone a Christian, but rather sharing in God's suffering in the worldly life" (portion of July 18, 1944 Bonhoeffer letter from prison to friend Eberhard Bethge).

It's important to remember that the fundamental temptation for us as human beings is to be less than human with despair and violence against humanity and creation or more than human with pride and violence against humanity and creation.

To simply be human, mortal and vulnerable and therefore true enough in a position to simply trust God (and, by extension, our homo sapiens sapiens place in the earth's ecology) rather than trust our subhuman groveling or superhuman machinations for who we are, where we belong, what is the meaning of our life and what will become of us…..to be simply and plainly and forthrightly human, something that Bonhoeffer says we are *allowed* to be, given the freedom to be (Galatians 5:1 "for freedom Christ has set me free") because of God's attitude and action toward us, to be human is what Christ does to us and gives to us and this understanding of who we are and who God is fundamental to understanding what Bonhoeffer is talking about with "religion-less Christianity." He is not, I remind you, talking about being "spiritual but not religious," as in the usual use of that phrase today where it means to believe in God (whatever that may mean!) but not like to participate in a religious organization's rituals and practices. He is rather talking about a following of Jesus ("Christianity") that does not *use God* to further our agency or agenda ("religion") but rather *trusts God* in all of our raw humanity, including of course, as if this needs to be said when it comes to being human, suffering and death.

And then let me put an even sharper edge on that "suffering and death": It's not that we only trust God when we are put upon (pain, illness, disease, death and not incidentally also the loneliness of losing loved ones) but that we trust God and we suffer God, we allow God to be God when our world turns godless, where God has left the building, where God does not in fact show up and fix anything. Do we see?

The accounting we have of Jesus is just that: the one who transforms all persons by loving at all costs (Jesus: "let me see….I'll feed you, heal you, raise you from the dead, just for starters, and then teach you like mad that life is about giving your life away and not holding on for dear life") simply up and dies (instead of fighting back against the Romans and Herodians or fleeing in order to fight another day). He doesn't change anything! And then there is this insult (to us) added to this injury: he comes back and rallies the troops for this same loving at all cost's way of life and then up and leaves again. And this time, for good! (I know, we have the hope of return and in fact I do hold that hope but after 2000 years I am not holding my breath). What kind of God does this!? We…. suffer……. this kind of God.

And it is precisely there, in that suffering that is our humanity, where we are not mired in despair, less than human, or elevated in pride, more than human, but rather fully human and living the way of the One who is the Way (this way of loving at all costs, even if it seems to do no earthly not so say also heavenly good) where we are met by God and find full life.

So, enough for this week. I do have to say I have a lot of thoughts about our national quagmire over gun violence and gun legislation and protection of freedoms and would love to share them and hear yours. How about if you join us at 11am-11:15am Sunday at our "Tracking Jesus Conversation Tables" where we simply listen to each other about how the weekly reading of Scripture in our daily prayer life (we are encouraging this project of having folks use the Revised Common Lectionary Daily Lectionary) is impacting us. Join in. In the Family Life Center. Well then this: I am going to tackle the gun violence through Mark 8 in preaching Sunday (see below). So come along, and let's let the Holy Spirit do something to us all.

In Life Together with you,

Pastor Johan

Life Together the week of February 25, 2018

What is this "religion-less Christianity" of which Bonhoeffer muses and writes and begins to formulate a vision?

It is more than and distinct from an anti-institutionalism of the spiritualism conveyed today. To grab hold of "being spiritual but not religious" can easily mean, and I think usually does, simply another form of religion cocooning itself away from creation and world. The only difference in the "cocooning" of religion that is "spiritual" as opposed to "religious" is that one does not participate in church worship or other traditional church activities.

Let me try to illustrate this "cocooning" or stepping away from the world or compartmentalizing the aspects of our life.

There is a thing called "The Wholeness Wheel" that graphically displays the vital components in our life as "slices of the pie" within this whole circle or pie.

The components or pieces of the pie: Vocational Wellness, Physical Wellness, Emotional Wellness, Social/Interpersonal Wellness, Financial Wellness, Intellectual Wellness. The key thing to see, however, with the Wheel, is that the circle, the ring around the pie, the thing that embraces all the components of the vital life, is called Spirituality or Spiritual Wellness. All the other "wellness" pieces are part of the definition of spiritual wellness. So, then, with that visual in mind, consider how too often folks consider "spirituality" as one piece of the pie along with all the other pieces in our life instead of the ring that encircles and embraces all of the pieces.

And then, with that approach of spirituality being one piece, those who are wont to consider themselves "spiritual but not religious" simply take that piece of the pie and drop the institution of church or other infrastructure they have carried around in their religious life. The spiritual is still only one piece of the life, not the whole, it just now has no religious organization, or at least traditional religious organization, underpinnings.

But notice what happens with "The Wholeness Wheel" where "spiritual wellness" encircles every aspect of the "pie" and is not just one slice of the "pie": all aspects of life, from cradle to grave, and all that is experienced in this life, are part and parcel of the faith. For me, this reflects Bonhoeffer's understanding of the "this worldliness" of the faith. It is a faith where "religion" is not one aspect of our life and the rest of our life is "the world" and all we necessarily need to engage. Religion is not one aspect of a whole where we retreat or find refuge or even where we advance and find empowerment. It simply is not a slice where we find God and thus encounter or embrace more of God's divinity for our humanity. It is not a religion-full Christianity. It rather is the whole pie, the whole experience of life, where we are in God and thus encounter and embrace more humanity on account of God's divinity. It is a religion-less Christianity.

To get a handle on the "full" and "less" aspects of religion as a descriptive of Christianity, then, one simply envisions the pie with its pieces, life with its components, and see that in the "religion-full" Christianity there is a "religion" piece of the pie to fill the pie (or, as I was trying to say above, for those who don't like "being religious," they simply replace this piece of the pie with "being spiritual," while still filling the pie with a piece of divine activity). In "religion-full" Christianity "religious" or "spiritual" are one piece of the pie. But, in a religion-less Christianity there is no "religion" piece in the pie (nor spiritual piece). That's the "less" aspect. Religion (religious or spiritual activity) is removed from simply being one dimension of a full life to rather being the thing that embraces and surrounds, informs and engenders, all aspects of life. It is the circle around the entire pie.

Enough for today. See below for Sunday's Taking the Message Home to prime the pump! Hope to see you around the Table!

In Life Together with you,

Pastor Johan

Life Together the week of March 11 2018

For those tracking Bonhoeffer's thinking and writing on "religion-less Christianity," August 3, 1944 is a big day**. Bonhoeffer wrote that day an "outline for a book," that he never got to write. Here we go with an excerpt:

> "Chapter 2:
>   (a) *Worldliness and God.*
>   (b) *Who is God? Not primarily a general belief in God's omnipotence and so on. That is not a genuine experience of God but just a prolongation of a piece of the world. Encounter with Jesus Christ. Experience that here there is a reversal of all human existence, in the very fact that Jesus only is 'there for others.' Jesus's 'being-for-others' is the experience of transcendence! Only through this liberation from self through this 'being-for-others' unto death, do*

> *omnipotence, omniscience, and omnipresence come into being. Faith is participating in this being of Jesus. (Becoming human, cross, resurrection.) Our relationship to God is no 'religious' relationship to some highest, most powerful, and best being imaginable – that is no genuine transcendence. Instead, our relationship to God is a new life in 'being there for others,' through participation in the being of Jesus. The transcendent is not the infinite, unattainable tasks, but the neighbor within reach in any given situation."*

As I think back over the last couple of years of my preaching with St. Philip I know I have spent a lot of energy trying to open up what Luther meant when he stated (Heidelberg Disputation) that we only know God through suffering and death.

There is a deep and abiding explosion of grace here that is hard for us to mine because we, could it be in fact innately, will not (not cannot, but will not.... see Luther's *Bondage of the Will*!), trust God because we will not allow ourselves to be simply and undeniably human, mortal, creatures who die and that's the end of our story.

The significant key to understanding Luther's "suffering and death" is to see that Luther is not talking about our active martyrdom but rather our passive acceptance that God is God and we are not. We suffer, we put up with, the fact that God does not do what we expect any decent card-carrying god to do: swoop in and save us from our foes, be they real or imaginary. Then this, to get us back to what Bonhoeffer is saying: we know all this about God and ourselves because of this Jewish man named Jesus.

Jesus, the very expression of God, so goes our confession, keeps us firmly grounded as humus, dust, earth, human. So now, in this place of humanity and there living only and there being in God, we find that the only true expression of living in God is to stay right here on earth and instead of looking up to know and experience divinity we literally look around and see where divinity lies: in our neighbors. Really? In Fernando, Joe, and Junior…. the crew that is installing my pavers on my porch today in my years in the making dream come true for a little slice of heaven on earth? Yes, these guys, and everybody else I know and meet. My neighbors.

And then, to put the finer point on it by making it whole, every creature, inanimate and animate in which I ecologically exist. Neighbors = creation.

But where is the "grace" here? How is this truth about best dust alone and eternally so and finding creation itself our home for which to care somehow liberating?

I can tell you why it is so for me: as I trudge many days, or like Oprah maybe even on some days wake up and first say "thank you," having the Spirit of God remind me (it's called metanoia, repentance, brought to me, not that I manufacture) that I have enough and I in fact, am enough, means the striving is over and the race is won and I'm not even close to finishing. Free to be. And that when the race is over, this life of mine let's call it, the song of life goes on without me.... because of......God. And so, to close, let me say again how we can come to such amazing conclusions about this dust and earth that we are and that God embraces and imbibes: Jesus.

Enough for today.

In Life Together with you,

Pastor Johan

Life Together the week of March 25 2018

Science, thankfully, has opened to us a world we can work with, not to say manipulate, for the betterment of all. Of course, we can use that same gain for worse. But that is another discussion. Here, I only speak of science in a neutral sense, a way of knowledge. And just at that fundamental level it has caused people of faith fits. This battle now, the battle between science and religion, was on a slow simmer for centuries but since the scientific method was "discovered" and employed in the Enlightenment it has been a raging fire. I am of the camp that it need not be so, that the two worlds of empirical data and spiritual engagement are not antithetical but in fact enrich each other. The collateral damage of this fire, but also perhaps the match that struck the flame, is the Christian's misuse of the Bible as a book of science (even as the Scientist has misused the laboratory as a place of faith).

So, we must use the Bible as a book of faith and not a book of fact. That in one key way will help us live in our world with intellectual honesty and live in faith as we engage our research in all scientific disciplines.

But there is something more, perhaps deeper and more fundamental that then too must happen even with that clarity of the co-relationship of faith and science, but perhaps too is revealed by this relationship. It is our understanding of how we know God, which is to say, how we live in faith.

Bonhoeffer writes to Eberhard Bethge on July 16, 1944 (*Letters and Papers from Prison*) that "*we cannot be honest unless we recognize that we have to live in the world – 'etsi deus non daretur'.*[23] *And this is precisely what we do recognize – before God! God himself compels us to recognize it. Thus our coming of age leads us to a truer recognition of our situation before God. God would have us know that we must live as those who manage their lives without God. The same God who is with us is the God who forsakes us (Mark 15:34!).*
The same God who makes us to live in the world without the working hypothesis of God is the God before whom we stand continually. Before God, and with God, we live without God. God consents to be pushed out of the world and onto the cross. God is

---

23 "as if there were no God"

weak and powerless in the world and in precisely this way, and only so, is at our side and helps us.

Matthew 8:17 24 makes it quite clear that Christ helps us not by virtue of this omnipotence but rather by virtue of his weakness and suffering! This is the crucial distinction between Christianity and all religions.
Human religiosity directs people in need to the power of God in the world as deus ex machina.25 The Bible directs people toward the powerlessness and the suffering God; only the suffering God can help. To this extent, one may say that the previously described development toward the world's coming of age, which has cleared the way by eliminating a false notion of God, frees us to see the God of the Bible, who gains ground and power in the world by being powerless. This will probably be the starting point for our 'worldly interpretation.'"

Bonhoeffer is unpacking something deep and wonderful here (and something, this "worldly interpretation," that he never got to finish!): science, with its uncompromising spotlight on evidence for truth has "cleared the way" for us to know a true notion of God:

---

24 referring to Isa. 53:4 "This was to fulfill what had been spoken through the prophet Isaiah: "He took our infirmities and bore our diseases.""

25 "the God from the machine." In the ancient theater this was a figure who could be made to appear suddenly with the help of a mechanical device and to solve problems supernaturally.

27*Heidelberg Disputation*, Thesis XXI, 1518.

to know God, as Luther put it: "God can be found only in suffering and the cross."26

Science, let us be clear, did not discover this, but perhaps did provide the bulldozer to plow away the piles and piles of theological rubble we in our human nature of wanting God to do what we want God to do when we want God to do it, have constructed: a God of power by victory through violence rather than a God of power by defeat through non-violence. This is a rubble we built way before any Renaissance or Enlightenment with their methods and insights.

Science, in other words, has provided this enormous side-benefit (besides inventing the toaster, sending us to the moon and curing malaria and….): it has allowed us to understand and live into the deep faith of knowing God only through radical reliance (trust) and radical obedience (love). Faith is not knowing God through any evidence, let alone the evidence that our status, security and safety have improved. Faith is knowing God through no evidence, and specifically the no evidence of a messiah who was killed and now, after showing up to vindicate love as the only way to live, has left the building.

It's Holy Saturday. The day of nothingness. The day of darkness. Saturday, March 31, 2018, Easter Vigil Day. A pretty good day to be engaging how God is here in this void.

I hope you can make it somewhere tomorrow around the Table as Christ himself in Bread and Wine is given to us all. It's Resurrection Day!

If you are in the Mt. Dora area, join us at 8:30am or 10:30am as God throws a party and we all show up to feast.

Life Together the week of April 1, 2018

What would become of our faith if we took away Sunday worship?

What if the church, the "called out ones," stopped producing worship services on Sunday morning?

To get to these questions, or one question, let's back up.

In his April 30, 1944 letter from prison to friend Eberhard Bethge, Bonhoeffer writes, in his first extant letter that specifically and denotatively dives into this notion of a religion-less Christianity:

"How do we talk about God – without religion, that is without the temporally conditioned presuppositions of metaphysics, the inner life, and so on? How do we speak (or perhaps we can no longer 'speak' the way we used to) in a 'worldly' way about God? How do we go about being 'religion-less-worldly' Christians, how can we be ecclesia (Greek: church, called-out ones), those who are called out, without understanding ourselves religiously as privileged, but instead seeing ourselves as belonging wholly to the world? Christ would no longer be the object of religion, but something else entirely, truly lord of the world. But what does that mean? In a religion-less situation, what do ritual (cultus) and prayer mean?

Is this where the arcane discipline' or the difference (which you've heard about from me before) between the penultimate and the ultimate, have new significance?"

It's hard for us (dare we say impossible, yes, we dare), perhaps sinfully so, in the sense of naturally so, which means in the sense of sin meaning we cannot, by nature, not think of ourselves first in all things, to put God at the center or to allow God to be at the center instead of at the periphery. (I recognize that to say it's 'impossible' ends the consideration if not to say also any discussion. But this "impossible talk" is to enter into the vital engaging of the nature of faith itself: that is not something that we produce but is something that is produced in us. There is a place where Jesus is quoted as saying "nothing is impossible with God" and this begins to get at it: for us to say something is impossible for us to do is not to say it's impossible for it to be done. This is a vital part of what it means to have faith, and must be left for another discussion. Right now, I will simply stick with "impossible" to describe our possibilities, not God's.)

It is impossible to allow God, thinking in terms of "The Wholeness Wheel" (where in the wheel are wellness aspects of our life: physical, intellectual, financial, emotional, social-interpersonal, vocational) to be the entire Wheel instead of a spoke in the wheel (the way that "spiritual" would be another dimension of wellness instead of the definition of wellness of all aspects combined).

Or let's make it "The Wholeness Pie" and speak of making God the whole Pie instead of a piece of the pie. But that is what a "religion-less Christianity" is: God is not a spoke in the wheel, but rather the Wheel. God is not a piece of the pie, but rather the Pie. It is God, Christ, as all there is. It is Christ as subject who acts on us rather than the object on whom we act.

I've often illustrated the place of worship and prayer, or all "spiritual practices," with the account of Gary Haugen and the organization he founded, International Justice Mission, as he told the story of how attorneys on the organization's staff that do the work of advocacy and action against human trafficking, must stop 2 times a day for 30 minutes of prayer and bible time because they simply cannot do the life and work of following Christ without Christ.

Prayer and devotion, here, we see, is not the last resort, a going to God to pull God in to help us do what we want to do, a going to God when all else fails, a turning to an aspect of reality that can assist the true reality or whole reality. It is rather a first resort, a going to God because God is all there is, because God is where we live.

So, back to the original questions today: what would become of our faith if we took away Sunday worship? What is the church, the called-out ones, stopped producing worship services on Sunday morning?

To imagine this brings us face to face with the vacuous nature of our faith and the actual nature of religion.

In Life Together with you,
Pastor Johan

Life Together the week of April 8 2018

How is there the power of God in Scripture? How can we teach and speak Scripture in a non-religious way, a religion-less way?

Dietrich Bonhoeffer from prison in 1944:

"It is not for us to predict the day – but the day will come – when people will once more be called to speak the word of God in such a way that the world is changed and renewed.

It will be in a new language, so that people will be alarmed and yet overcome by its power – the language of a new righteousness and truth, a language that proclaims God makes peace with humankind and that God's kingdom is drawing near."

Let's remember that "the word of God" is first of all the person of Jesus, secondly, what Jesus does to us (command and promise, law and gospel), and thirdly, the written Bible.

That being said, let me share something about the relationship of Jesus and the Bible accounts about him and his followers and try then to say something about how this "new language" of which Bonhoeffer speaks is happening now.

I have some reflections on Acts 4 (go ahead and read it now) and Jesus. I'm calling this: "Jesus Changes Everything." Here we go.
It's important to read the New Testament through the lens of what actually killed Jesus and what it meant to declare that his way now still lives, his life now still lives, and is the standard operating procedure for personal and community life. How else can you explain that the authorities wanted to suppress Peter and the others? If by declaring Jesus "was the name by which all were to be saved" simply meant a declaration of personal piety of heart allegiance to a Spiritual Being, this could be tolerated by civic and

political authorities in a "tolerance of all religions" approach that was subservient to the authority of Rome and the Herodians.

This would be much like Pilate tolerated Jewish piety and ritual, even Temple observances, and the Sanhedrin did the same, as long as any religious observance did not challenge the economic and political control (hegemony some might say!) they enjoyed from cooperation with Rome. A cult of followers of this Jesus from Nazareth who was no longer on the scene would easily have been allowed as long as it kept its business to personal and internal spiritual matters and not communal and external matters. But this Jesus movement picked up where Jesus left off: challenging the oppression with a new culture of distributive justice. See in Acts 4 the radical sharing of resources this Jesus community espoused and lived out. And their message was that Jesus, allegiance to and trust in Jesus, is what drives this way of living. Their message was that Jesus changes the way we live. Their message was that Jesus changes lives. Their message was that Jesus changes everything.

Their message was that Jesus saves. And, by the way, no one else does (again, see Acts 4).

But know this, this "no one else" thing is not some proposition of exclusive privilege with which you too could gain access if you but believe it (the 20th century, western world culture theology that has made Christianity into a religious belief system to which one must ascribe in order to live after you die). It was rather a statement of fact: no one else, besides Jesus and his now "born again" community, was doing this! No one else was living like this: allegiance to God and justice for all, peace by distributive justice through non-violence. It was the only name and game in town doing this! Jesus' name, and living in his name, was the only name by which to be saved!

How can you read this account in Acts 4 and then of course the rest of the story and growth and development of the Jesus movement, church, in Acts, and not be bewildered by how we have domesticated the faith and missed the explosion of this radical life of living in Jesus, but also be enlivened by what is possible if we unearthed (Resurrection!) the faith and unleashed the faith to encounter our challenges of conflict, war, poverty and environmental degradation?

When Jesus lives he lives not only in your heart but in the streets. And by that, I mean not only non-violent marching but non-violent living in workplace and home and all civic life.

Christ is risen! Let's get on with it!

Okay, with that bit of reflection on Acts 4 and Jesus, do we see what is possible if we let the accounts of Scripture live as they really are: they are a theology about actual history, they are not history about actual theology. Seeing Scripture and engaging Scripture in this way will allow us to then speak of God and in God with non-religious language.

The world is dying to hear a word of hope.

The world is dying for lack of a way to live non-violently.

Let's bring what we know. Let's bring Jesus so that, as Bonhoeffer wrote, "the world is changed and renewed."

In Life Together with you,

Pastor Johan

Fate

Life Together the week of April 15 2018

What if there is no plan?

All my years as a pastor I have heard people say as they try to figure rhyme and reason for what they are engaging, be it disaster or delight, "it must be a part of God's plan," or "it is God's plan," or "there is a reason for everything." When we can't figure out what's going on or can see clearly what's going on but are happy about it and must attribute it to a Higher Power or are unhappy about it and must do the same, we give God the space, the benefit of the doubt, the recognition and attribution if not too the glory.

But what if there is no plan?

We become a bit uneasy, perhaps even unnerved, if we get the notion or the feeling that what is happening to us and around us is random, and, of course that what is happening by us, the actions we take and accomplish, have no truck with the divine or supernatural and have simply the temporal consequences that are readily seen, or alas, not seen and we wonder what we are doing it all for anyway.

If life is random and Darwinian, what place does God have in our life? What claim does God have on our life, if there is no plan?

Let me just say it. I do not believe God has a plan for my life. I do believe in God, but I do not believe God has a plan for my life or for the world. What must be also said at the same time, however, is that by saying no to a plan but yes to God means to say I believe there is the operative and real guiding principle of peace, shalom, by distributive justice through non-violence (all of which is to say: unconditional love) and that this way of being, this love, is most clearly revealed and definitely made operational in the person of Jesus of Nazareth.

I remember well the time, years ago while as seminary intern, I sat in a plenary session at a Church District Youth Gathering (it was the old Southeastern District of the American Lutheran Church and it was in North Carolina) when then Bishop Harold Jansen asked this large gathering of high school young people, many trying to figure out what to do after high school, all simply trying to navigate the vicissitudes of adolescence with its "who am I?" and "How do I fit in?" questions, this question: What does God say to you regarding what you are to do with your life? When you ask God what you supposed to do with your life, what is God telling you? I'll tell you what God is telling you, God is telling you: "Surprise me!"

Really? That's what God is going to tell me? That's what God is telling me? There is no plan and I need to make this up as I go along? Doesn't that mean that God doesn't care? Or this: doesn't that mean that there s no God?

Living with such an answer requires faith (a trust in the relationship with the divine, not in how well we are doing with tactics) and grit (perseverance and passion in getting on with what you have and feel called to do).

We can see that believing in God, and more specifically believing that God is revealed in Jesus for the sake of the blessing and healing of the world, and not believing there is a plan for me or you or even for the world for that matter, requires a different kind of believing in God than we are used to engaging.

Dietrich Bonhoeffer, while in prison for witnessing to Christ through the Confessing Church and not the National Socialist Church, being a political operative in rescuing Jews from Nazi pogroms, and then ultimately executed April 9, 1945 by the Nazi regime for participating in the failed plot to assassinate Hitler in July 1944, was writing letters and theological papers on what it meant to follow Jesus in "a world come of age," a world where religion has been boxed up and placed outside of the natural world and only called on to intervene supernaturally when the natural world got out of hand and did not go according to plan.

He was not arguing that religion had to be unboxed and placed back in the natural world in order to explain or make sense of the natural world, something that religion had been trying to do since the dawn of the scientific method, but that rather religion had to take a new place, its rightful place in relationship with world: religion was not a part or parcel of the world, but rather was the world itself, that all things, including science, are within God. Because we get uneasy or anxious with the natural world being the operating force ("random acts of God" are actually random acts of nature) religion works hard, and earns its keep, by explaining just how the supernatural impacts the natural and how we should all pay attention to the supernatural if we know what is good for us. Bonhoeffer was working on describing how God is real and significant and indeed impactful as the operating force of the natural world and not an invading force of the supernatural world on the natural world

Here is Bonhoeffer while in prison on July 8, 1944 to friend Eberhard Bethge:

"What I am driving at is that God should not be smuggled in somewhere, in the very last, secret place that is left. Instead, one must simply recognize that the world and humankind have come of age. One must not find fault with people in their worldliness but rather confront them with God where they are the strongest. One must give up the 'holier-than-thou' ploys and not regard psychotherapy or existential philosophy as scouts preparing the way for God.
The intrusive manner of all these methods is far too unaristocratic for the Word of God to be allied with them. The Word of God does not ally itself with this rebellion of mistrust, this rebellion from below. Instead, it reigns"

I'm not sure where this leaves me today. Remember, please, I write this stuff for Life Together as it hits me and do not try to make coherent sense......that may come later if I try to pull together these forays into "religion-less Christianity." Let me simply say that having no divine plan for my life doesn't make it harder to explain or experience life, but rather, actually easier and better. Jesus is the Christ and simply invites us to follow. I will go there.

In Life Together with you,

Pastor Johan

Life Together the week of April 29 2018

This past Thursday at the National Day of Prayer celebration about 100 folks gathered at Annie Donnelly Park in downtown Mt. Dora and lots of prayers were prayed. One prayer caught my heart as the leader prayed thanks for the creation, and for us as being creation too, of God, but then he went on to say thank you for us created by God being made a new creation in Christ. He's correct, of course, and spot on biblically: "so if anyone is in Christ there is a new creation, everything old has passed away" (2 Corinthians 5).

But this is precisely where we turn the wrong corner, usually, with the faith. This transformation, what is it? What changes? How is the creature new because of Christ?

Dietrich Bonhoeffer writes on July 18, 1944 to Eberhard Bethge (in one of the letters most spiced with "religion-less" Christianity thinking): "Being a Christian does not mean being religious in a certain way, making oneself into something or other (a sinner, penitent, or saint) according to some method or other. Instead, it means being human, <u>not a certain type of human being</u>, but the human being Christ creates in us" (see too *Life Together* the week of January 25, 2018).

[margin note: The Christ self]

[margin note: The way of the world is evolution — survival of the fittest — Included in us — opposite of Christ's way.]

The wrong turn we take with "new creation" is thinking that in Christ we are now different than human if not more than human. The correct turn: the "human being that Christ creates in us" is the one that being born in flesh and blood actually is.

Being "born again" (to use a phrase!) does not mean to get beyond, now, our skin, but to be <u>comfortable</u> in our skin, skin being not only the only thing we have but also the only thing we need.

[margin note: N.t it]

Our "problem," if that's what we can call it, is that we don't like who and what we are: mortal skin and bones. Human. We cannot allow ourselves to be here and gone, to not be the center (of the universe), to not exist. (Promise that we will

We are bothered, we recoil, indeed, we lash out against, someone else being the center being the main thing, being immortal.

What Christ does is knock us off the high horse of pride and brings us back to our humanity and what Christ does is lift us up from the dregs of our despair and brings us back to our humanity. Jesus was not blowing smoke when he called us to trust God and love neighbor.

In other words, regarding that first part on "trusting God", to allow God to take care of our created selves instead of pridefully inventing projects, spiritual or otherwise, to take care of ourselves, or despairingly throwing in the towel over our frailties and foibles, is possible. We confess as Christians that Christ does this to us and for us.

How is all of this "religion-less Christianity?"

Religion is a spiritual construction project we initiate, manage and complete. Christianity is a human life experience we receive and live within.

Religion says a new creation is no longer creation. Christianity says a new creation is only and ever will be creation.

In Life Together with you,

Pastor Johan

Life Together the week of May 13 2018

I used to think Augustine had it right when he wrote *"You have made us for yourself, O Lord, and our heart is restless until it rests in you."* (St. Augustine's Confessions (Lib 1,1-2,2.5,5: CSEL 33, 1-5). Well, I still think he's right, but I wonder if we don't approach understanding it from a Self-Centered (note, not selfish necessarily, but Self as Center) rather than God-Centered point of view and throw it off kilter. It may be true, but not if it means that we are built, created, in some way to be just fine without God, thank you very much, until we find we have needs and it is then in those needs that we can go looking for God and God is there, albeit out of divine goodness, to oblige. We are not made to find our rest in God in the sense that we are whole without God but then we find we are not whole, somehow, and God is there to fill the hole, fill the gap.

Instead, this: We are made, period. And there is God, period. In this order of creation and Creator there is order and stability and there is wholeness and in all of this there is a rest, a way that things should be. And this rest, the place of stability of being a created being who trusts the Creator implicitly, there is no place nor room for religion. Nobody needs to be religious, acting upon God or attempting transactions with God in order to make things right.

Things go right and things go wrong, and in all these things there is simply a created being who lives with all of that and a Creator who embraces all of that.

In the sense that we are created beings, human beings, who have no need to call upon God to do something for us or be for us because we are in fact created by God and God never turns away or spurns God's creation, it is in this sense that we are what Augustine says "you have made us for yourself."

But we just can't buy this. We can't do what I said above: "implicitly trust the creator." We can't not have a need to call upon God to do for us what we want rather than simply see God, listen to God, and do what God wants. This is the essence of sin: to not trust the Creator and instead create the project of religion.

Bonhoeffer wrote of a "world come of age" where God was pushed out of the equation of life as the one who came to the rescue, was a God who came to fill the gaps of knowledge and experience, and Bonhoeffer did not bemoan this world. He welcomed it.

But he asked then the hard question: what does it mean to believe in God when God is real and has agency upon us, impact upon us, but not in order to fill in incomplete information or incomplete experience? What if we have all the information and all the experience and we are very strong? And, simultaneously, what if God is, well God (which means, we are not!)?

Bonhoeffer saw in Jesus of Nazareth God encountering humanity in humanity's strength, not weakness, and calling on that strength to be about the business of God (peace by justice through non-violence). This is a world and way that does not create or live by religion: using belief or behavior to get God to do what we need God to do. This is a world and way that lives by God: letting

Do we have agency to do good?

ourselves be shaped by God to do what God wants to do and what God needs us to do. In calling for a "religion-less Christianity" note there is a Christianity.

It's not a call for kicking out God of our understanding or our lives and how we engage life. It's a call to have God take the proper place: engaging all of humanity and creation, science and all.

In Life Together with you,

Pastor   Johan

Made in the USA
Columbia, SC
15 October 2018